W9-BGF-479

BLOOD, MONEY, &GREED

The Money Trust Conspiracy

BLOOD, MONEY, &GREED

The Money Trust Conspiracy

CLIFF FORD

WESTERN FRONT

Library of Congress Catalog Card Number:
98–060851

ISBN 1–888848–23–5

Published by WESTERN FRONT LTD., Beverly Hills, CA

Interior design by Koechel Peterson & Associates,
Minneapolis, Minnesota

Manufactured in the United States of America

CONTENTS
• • •

CHAPTER 4—DOING THE WASH 81

Making Dirty Money Clean... CREEP... No Game for Amateurs
Money Laundering as a Concept... The Tracking System
Case in Point... Passing the Buck... Bankers with Bent Noses
BCCI and the London Connection

CHAPTER 5—THE POLITICS OF WAR 97

The Middle East Conflict... Dollars and Sense... Origin of the Peace
Process... Drums of War... The Growing European–Arab Connection
The Banker's War... The Roots of Conflict... Legacy of the Gulf War
Weapons of Peace... The Syrian Threat... Egypt's Military Buildup
Chemical Weapons... Biological Weapons... Iran—The Joker in the Deck
Neutralizing America... A European Russian Axis?... Russia's Angle

CHAPTER 6—THE NEW MONEY 117

Setting the Stage... Will That Be Debit or Charge?
Enter the Internet System... How Did That Happen?
The Next Global Power Isn't Political... The New "Global Power"
Who Runs the New Europe?... $$$ Makes the World Go 'Round
Politics vs. Economics... A Good King or a Bad King?

CHAPTER 7—THE RING OF FIRE 131

Dictators R Us... The Ring of Fire... The Hong Kong Handover
The Big Picture... The Biggest Market in the World... Money Is a Weapon
Wealth Equals Power... The UK's on First. China's on Third.
Who's on Second?... Asleep at the Switch... A Paper Tiger
Japan's Loose Cannon... Countdown to Meltdown
The Great Bailout of 1997... Who Is the World Bank?
Eliminating the Competition... Mega Banks... The Politics of the Bailout
And Here's How... Let the (Blue) Chips Fall Where They May

CHAPTER 8—WALL STREET 159

The 1997 Fender Bender... History Fails to Repeat Itself... What's the Plan?
Whose Money Is Behind It All?... From the Oval Office... Partners in Fact
What's in a Word?... Inflation, the Stock Market and the Price of Vegetables
In Boise... A Deflationary Tale... Not Everybody Takes a Beating

CHAPTER ONE

THE HISTORY OF MONEY

"The Government should create, issue, and circulate

all the currency and credits needed to satisfy the spending power

of the Government and the buying power of consumers.

By the adoption of these principles, the taxpayers

will be saved immense sums of interest.

Money will cease to be master

and become the servant of humanity."

ABRAHAM LINCOLN

CONSPIRACY OR MYTH?

We hear a lot in the news about conspiracies and evil men secretly planning the takeover of the world. In the conventional sense, it is highly unlikely. But there is a money trust, and it is no secret. *TIME* listed the ten most powerful men in the world in a recent issue.

First was the President of the United States, but he was one of only two politicians on the list. After him came the CEO of Microsoft, then the chairman of the Fed, then the CEO's of various multinational corporations and global media conglomerates. Bringing up a distant tenth on the list is the man who is supposed to be the second most powerful man on earth, the Speaker of the House of Representatives, Newt Gingrich. Almost as if Clinton and Gingrich were "token" politicians put there to assure us the democratic process still had some influence over the global power structure.

But it is the guys with the gold who make the rules. Do you doubt me? Consider this. If a so–called "money trust" were merely the creation of overactive imaginations among late 20th century conspiracy buffs, the trail would begin and end in the late 20th century. But it does not. Let's take a look at the historical record. It may seem a little dull, but that is the money trust's strength. As long as it is too boring for the uninitiated, the guys pulling the strings can operate out in the open without fear. So bear with me.

THE HISTORY OF MONEY

One would assume that once money was invented, the concept of banking evolved as a method of handling that money. In reality, banking came first. Money was an invention of banking! The invention of banking preceded that of coinage, or money. Banking originated in Ancient Mesopotamia where the royal palaces and temples provided secure places for the safe–keeping of grain and other commodities. Receipts came to be used for transfers not only to the original depositors but also to third parties. Eventually, private houses in Mesopotamia also got involved in these banking operations and laws regulating them were included in the code of Hammurabi. Those receipts were the first paper money. Paper money has always been representative of something of value, a token completely devoid of any intrinsic value of its own. A person would exchange a receipt for grain on deposit in exchange for goods or services. Historically, it was a barter system. The receipt could be "cashed in"—and that is what gave it value.

Grain as money was not entirely satisfactory, however. It wasn't very durable, and during periods of famine, there wasn't enough available to put into storage. No grain meant no receipts, and that meant no money. A more reliable base for measuring wealth was necessary.

Precious metals, in weighed quantities, became a common form of money. The transition to quantities that could be counted rather than weighed came gradually. The words "spend," "expenditure," and "pound" (as in the main British monetary unit) all come from the Latin *expendere,* meaning "to weigh." The basic unit of weight in the Greek speaking world was the "drachma" or "handful" of grain, but the precise weight taken to represent this varied considerably. Throughout much of the ancient world, the basic unit of money was the stater, meaning literally "balancer" or "weigher." The talent is a monetary unit with which we are

familiar from the Parable of the Talents in the Bible. The
talent was also a Greek unit of weight, about 60 pounds.

Historically, money was an expression of wealth, a measure
of tangible wealth that could be weighed and measured. To
give it stability, money's value was pegged to a standard-
ized measure of a substance of universal value. The name of
the currency unit denoted the weight of the substance of
value: talent, drachma, pound, etc. Banks served as guarantors; they attested to the fact the monetary unit was in fact a
representation of real wealth stored by them on deposit.
Therefore, any person holding a receipt for a measure of
wealth could have confidence that receipt would be
exchanged on demand for the wealth it represented.

SOMETHING FOR NOTHING

In medieval societies, the receiver of deposits of wealth
was usually the local goldsmith. By virtue of his trade, he
was in the best position to guard the wealth of the community. Gold and silver were locked away in his vault, and a
warehouse receipt was issued. The goldsmith would charge
a small fee for storing the wealth which was deducted
before the receipt was issued. The receipt was redeemable
at its face value on demand. The community's confidence
in the value of the receipt was directly related to their confidence in the integrity of the issuer. As deposits grew,
greater numbers of transactions were completed by the
exchange of these warehouse receipts. They became "as
good as gold." The keepers of the gold noticed that the gold
in storage remained more or less constant. As long as confidence in the receipts remained high, there was always
more gold in the vault than there were receipts presented

for payment. The goldsmiths could safely issue more receipts for gold than the amount on deposit—in effect, creating money out of nothing. The effect was that each fraudulent receipt reduced the value of the gold on deposit by the amount of the bogus receipt issued. But as long as there wasn't a "run on the bank"—that is, as long as everybody didn't show up at the same time, the thefts would remain undiscovered.

BIRTH OF FRACTIONAL RESERVE BANKING

Our goldsmiths branched out into the loan business, following the same principle. They would lend gold, in the form of paper receipts, at interest, and take title to real property as collateral. The gold they lent was not theirs, it was the property of the depositors. Provided there was enough gold to cover any receipts presented for payment, there was no problem. This laid the foundation of a fractional reserve monetary system, and our goldsmiths became bankers.

By reducing or expanding the number of receipts in circulation, they could artificially manipulate the economy. A reduction in receipts in circulation created an economic depression. Bankers confiscated the collateral of those who defaulted on loans. Do you see how it works? Bankers created money out of nothing in the form of loans against which victims pledged real property. If the loan was repaid, the banker reaped a profit from money that did not exist in the form of interest. If the loan went into default, the banker took possession of real wealth by writing off as a loss money that didn't exist in the first place!

BIRTH OF THE SHADOW GOVERNMENT

The American Revolution was fought over money as much as any other cause. In particular, over who would control the American money supply. The British at first restricted, then forbade, the colonists to issue their own money. When he was in London in 1766, Benjamin Franklin tried in vain to convince Parliament of the need for a general issue of colonial paper money, but to no avail. The London banking establishment had no desire to lose its stranglehold on the banking monopoly it enjoyed in the colonies.

Two hundred and twenty–one years ago, the British crown made a power grab, hoping to take control of the largest emerging free market in the world at that time. The original 13 colonies founded by English settlers grew beyond the wildest dreams of even the most optimistic investors in the New World. The potential wealth was enormous, but the settlers wanted to control that wealth themselves. England was prepared to be accommodating, until Benjamin Franklin announced the colonists' plans to create their own central bank of issue. The American War for Independence began, therefore, not so much over political self determination, as over who would control that wealth.

THE RED SHIELD

The British crown arranged through Mayer Amshel Bauer to purchase an army of mercenary soldiers, the Hessians, to fight on the British side. The Americans won, the British lost, but Mayer Amshel Bauer learned an important lesson. It doesn't matter who wins or who loses. Wars cost money, and there are big profits to be made. Mayer Amshel Bauer changed his last name to "Rothschild" after the red shield on the door of the house he shared with the Schiff family in Frankfurt, Germany. By 1812, Rothschild was worth one billion francs. His five sons founded banks in Paris, London, Austria and Germany. The third son, Nathan, was soon the most powerful banker in England. By 1812, he was the undisputed head of the Bank of England. To England, the outcome of the Napoleonic War was critical both politically and economically. Nobody recognized that more clearly than Nathan Rothschild. If Napoleon had won, England's economic woes would be just beginning. England had borrowed huge sums of money for the prosecution of that war. England's international prestige was on the line, as well as its bank balance. Her defeat would also mean she would be unable to pay off her huge war debts, most of which were held by the Rothschild interests. The Rothschilds were already well–respected, not only for their financial acumen, but also for their ability to find things out. It was well known in financial circles that they maintained an efficient private courier service. If there was something big happening in the world of high finance, Nathan knew it first. And everybody knew it. It was therefore not surprising that all eyes were on Rothschild on June 20, 1815. News had already reached England that Napoleon's armies began massing for battle outside Waterloo two days before. But the outcome was still in question. In the early hours of June 20, 1815, an exhausted Rothschild courier named Rothworth gave Nathan the news. Victory was England's!

That morning, Lord Rothschild took up his usual place by the pillar at the Exchange and began to sell. The "smart" money interpreted his move as confirmation that Napoleon had won, and that their British securities would soon be worthless. Everybody began to sell, and prices plummeted. Eventually, prices collapsed altogether. Rothschild made his move, reversing his call, and cornered the entire market in government bonds. In a few hours, he had accumulated the bulk of England's entire debt for a tiny fraction of its value.

All five sons recognized the big money came, not from home equity loans, but from loaning money to governments. Nathan's first big loan to the British government came in 1819, a loan worth $60 million. Over the next 12 years, he loaned the Crown another $105,400,000. All told, by 1836, the Crown was in hock to Nathan Meyer Rothschild to the tune of $700 million—an enormous sum at the time. All five Rothschild banks prospered as bankers to the crowned heads of Europe. So much so that the *New York Times* wrote; "The Rothschilds introduced the rule of money into European politics. The Rothschilds were the servants of money who undertook to reconstruct the world as an image of money and its functions. Money and the employment of wealth have become the law of European life; we no longer have nations, but economic provinces." The power such wealth could buy was so great that another New York paper was of the opinion, "The Kaiser had to consult Rothschild to find out whether or not he could declare war."

WHAT IS "LAWFUL US MONEY"?

After the Revolution, the European Houses of Rothschild saw an opportunity to seize control of the emerging United States. Nathan Rothschild observed at the time: "Give me control of a nation's currency, and I care not who makes its laws." There were a couple of problems, however. The US

Constitution put control of the nation's currency in the hands of Congress, and made no provision for Congress to delegate that authority. It even established the basic currency unit, the dollar. The Dutch had considerable influence during the early colonization of the New World, particularly in New York. So, when Congress named the new American unit, it was based on the Dutch measurement—the thaler. The thaler was a specific weight of silver or gold coin. The Currency Act of 1792 (which has never been repealed) defines a dollar as 412.5 grains of 9/10s fine silver[1] (see pp. 33–35). Federal Reserve notes are not redeemable in silver. So a Federal Reserve note is not a dollar in lawful US money.

Those provisions were designed to keep the American money supply out of the hands of the banking industry. The Bank of England made several attempts to usurp control of the US money supply. The First Bank of the United States was chartered by the Bank of England in 1791 to finance the war debt of the Revolutionary War. It was abolished by Congress in 1811.

Along came the War of 1812 followed by the Second Bank of the United States, also chartered by the Bank of England to carry the American war debt. When its charter expired in 1836, President Andrew Jackson refused to renew it, saying a central bank concentrated too much power in the hands of unelected bankers. The Rothschild Bank of England immediately divested itself of all its American holdings. By refusing credit to American notes and stocks, the Bank of England caused a financial panic, known to history as the Panic of 1837. The depression enabled the Rothschild operations to buy up depreciated stocks for just pennies on the dollar.

BACKING THE WRONG HORSE

During the Civil War, England supported the Confederacy because it was promised a central bank charter, provided Jefferson Davis's Confederate states emerged victorious from the conflict.

President Lincoln stubbornly refused to let Rothschild interests finance the Union, instead issuing his famous "greenbacks," paper money backed, not by gold, but by the credit of the United States. It was a temporary measure, and "greenbacks" traded at many times below their face value in exchange for gold coin. It was the first and last effort by the legal, elected government of the United States to counterfeit its own money. Meanwhile, back in England, it seemed the only way for European banks to insinuate themselves into the American economy was by becoming American. The Rothschild interests in London underwrote the investment firm of Morgan–Grenfell as one of its confidential financial agents. It was headed by American expatriate Junius P. Morgan. His son, J. P. Morgan, turned it into an American dynasty and an agent of the London Rothschild family, as we shall see.

The period between the War Between the States and the birth of the Federal Reserve was marked by repeated and carefully planned crises designed to convince America that a new kind of banking system was necessary to protect us from cut-throats, pirates and currency speculators of all stripes.

The National Banking Acts of 1863 and 1865 conditioned the public to the notion that a system of federally chartered banks was not an economic cartel—even though there is no other accurate way of describing such a creature. The feder-ally chartered banking system was granted a monopoly in the issuance of bank notes as a substitute for silver and gold coin. Under the charter, the US government bound itself—and its citizens—to accept notes issued by these banks at face value. The charter meant that even banks whose own positions were somewhat shaky could issue bank notes that were federally guaranteed. In effect, the National Banking Act put into action the principles of central banking that would culminate half a century later as the Federal Reserve System.

BUSTS, BOOMS AND BANKERS

In order to make sure the American people really got the message, the economy underwent four major contractions of the money supply. As we saw earlier, these contractions were called "panics"—mainly because that was the term that best suited the situation. If a person were to shout "Fire!" in a crowded movie theater, the rush to get out would create something of a panic. People have been known to be trampled to death as they fled in the crush to get out and save themselves. A financial panic follows the same principle. A person "in the know" shouts "Fire!" at the right moment, and a panic ensues as investors try to save their holdings from being consumed. Along the way, a few are trampled to death financially. The cooler heads in the crowd merely wait until all the lemmings have fled and pick up the pieces—usually for pennies on the dollar. The panics of 1873, 1884, 1893, and 1907 served a dual purpose. Not only did they enable the insiders to increase their wealth and power, but the panics served to raise the cry "Something must be done!" so that they could appear on the scene just in time to rescue the economy. The principle that America required an economic Messiah figure gradually took shape as the survivors picked up what was left of their shattered holdings.

It had become a matter of faith that these panics were caused by seasonal demands for agricultural loans, especially at harvest time. There is some truth to the myth. To service rural banks, the larger banks would find themselves short of cash to meet industrial needs. As the cash reserves thinned for industry, large manufacturers would grow uneasy. Big city banks would restrict the flow of cash to the isolated farm communities. Soon, the whole system would weaken or collapse. But there was a flaw in the logic that seems apparent in hindsight. The panics only took place every decade or so. One doesn't need a slide rule and a degree in astrophysics to recognize that there is at least one harvest season every year. It didn't come on suddenly; it happened as regularly as, well, as seasons. So why didn't the banking establishment make provisions for adequate cash in advance of the demand? And why would the mere refusal to grant loans to farms, or industry, for that matter, turn into a panic every year?

Obviously, the panics weren't panics at all. They were just a smoke screen to impress upon the public the need for a central banking system. They had to be periodic. If there was a "panic" every year, then it wouldn't be a panic, just a seasonal money shortage. People would make allowances in advance for the shortage, even if the banks didn't, but that would upset the Plan.

THE MAGICIANS

Although these periods of restricted money cut across all economic lines, there always seemed to be just a few people that never got burned. They seemed to have some kind of magic charm. A few privileged banking families always seemed to have their holdings somewhere else when an ill wind was blowing their way. One of the most "fortunate" families was the House of Morgan.

The House of Morgan was actually founded by an American merchant from Massachusetts named George Peabody. In 1837, he made a trip to England to try and round up investors for the Chesapeake Ohio Canal project. He didn't receive a very warm welcome among most British investment houses. After meeting with outright opposition from much of the British banking establishment, Peabody opened an import–export business on Old Broad Street in London and began to provide banking services, letters of credit and loans to many of his shippers. Soon after he arrived in London, Peabody was summoned to an audience with Baron Nathan Meyer Rothschild. Rothschild recognized he was not entirely popular with London's aristocracy and proposed that Peabody be established as his proxy to represent his interests in secret. Rothschild backed Peabody financially in return for a promise that Peabody would serve as one of the House of Rothschild's most important secret agents. A strong anti–Semitic and anti–Rothschild sentiment had grown up in Europe and America, and the family often found it to its advantage to work through agents rather than deal directly. Eventually, Peabody found himself numbered among London's investment bankers, specializing in transactions between Britain and the United States. As his business grew and prospered, his firm found itself in an unusually prime position to exploit what was, at the time, a rapidly expanding market. Peabody never married, and as he approached retirement, he began to look for someone to carry on his business. It was not an easy order to fill. The successful candidate had to be American, but he also had to be acceptable to old British money. The British upper crust still sniffed at Americans as "renegade colonials." To fit in, the candidate had to be of sufficient breeding and with sufficient education in all the right schools to fit into London's closed social circles. He had to know enough about both the British and American financial systems to be able to not just survive, but prosper the firm.

PEABODY BECOMES MORGAN

In 1850, George Peabody met Junius P. Morgan at a London dinner party. Morgan impressed Peabody immediately, and Peabody began to take an interest in young Morgan's background. The meeting resulted in a relationship that brought Junius Morgan into the firm as a full partner in 1854. The firm was soon known as Peabody, Morgan, and Company. Ten years later, George Peabody retired, and the firm immediately began doing business as J. S. Morgan and Company. His son, John Pierpont Morgan, was educated at the English High School in Boston, but enrolled in European schools of higher education to round out his background. John Pierpont Morgan excelled in his father's business, branching out the family firm, eventually setting up a New York branch in partnership with Anthony Drexel of Philadelphia. Drexel, Morgan, and Company did business from 1871 to 1895. When Drexel died in 1895, the firm of J. P. Morgan & Company of New York brought the House of Morgan full circle from London to New York—a thoroughly American banking firm.

PANIC, WHAT PANIC?

During the Wall Street Panic of 1857, many US buyers were unable to pay their bills, and Peabody and Morgan were expected to make good on their guarantees. Peabody and Morgan didn't have the money, either, but they knew where they could get it. According to Stanley Jackson's biography of J. P. Morgan:

> "The clouds lifted dramatically when the Bank of England announced a loan to Peabody's of 800,000 pounds, at very reasonable interest, with the promise of further funds up to a million sterling if and when required. It was a remarkable vote of confidence as Thomas Hankey (governor of the Bank of England) had already rejected similar appeals from various American firms who did not measure up to his standards."

Presumably, those "standards" included the direct support of the House of Rothschild, to whom such sums were mere pocket change.

That is only one story out of several dozen, but it is representative of the manner in which the banking elite of the Federal Reserve owe their allegiances to the London banking establishment backed by the House of Rothschild. There are many others, but space is limited and there is still much to discuss. Suffice to say Brown Bros. (now Brown Brothers–Harriman) was also a creation of the Rothschild European interests in 1835. The Rothschild European banks financed many other American dynasties like the Rockefeller family and "Americanized" European banking houses like Kuhn, Loeb Co., J. M. Schroeder, Jacob Schiff, etc.

KING GEORGE WON, AFTER ALL—SORT OF

Once free of the British banking system, the Founding Fathers had no desire to become slaves to another.

As I said earlier, the Constitution explicitly gave Congress the responsibility for regulating the money supply and set up a monetary standard similar to the drachma or pound, but uniquely American. It established the dollar as a measure of a specific weight of silver struck into a silver coin. Gold was valued according to a formula of dollars of silver per ounce of gold. The dollar was not money. This can't be stressed strongly enough! Silver and gold coins were money, as established by the United States Constitution. The dollar was merely an expression of a specific weight of precious metal.

The US was founded under a barter system, similar to that of ancient times. A dollar was a weight of silver. Two dollars were twice that amount. A $20 gold coin weighed twice as much as a $10 gold coin. And inflation was impossible, because you could not create money out of nothing. There was no substitute for gold and silver coin. Prices remained as constant as the money supply.

THE CENTRAL BANKING SYSTEM

Bankers didn't much care for this system, so they began issuing their own scrip—receipts for gold on deposit, just like the goldsmiths of old. Bankers got rich under the credit system they created. The government did not, due to the honest nature of the barter system.

The banking establishment made several attempts to create a central banking system in the United States, but the US officially remained on a gold–backed barter economy for 137 years, until 1913, when the Federal Reserve was created. The banking industry had their central bank!

The Fed is a privately owned banking system run for profit. It is not a government agency. Its officers are not government officials. The Federal Reserve Act replaced the American barter economy with that of a fractional reserve—the same system used by our goldsmith to create money out of nothing, using that "phantom" money to expropriate real property.

The Fed was supposed to regulate the banking system to prevent panics and fluctuations in the money supply. It set out to do that by replacing real money—silver and gold coin—with Federal Reserve Notes—receipts issued against gold on deposit. Is this starting to sound familiar?

WHO NEEDS GOLD?

The Crash of '29 (an event that the Fed was supposed to prevent) resulted in the Great Depression. Remember how our goldsmith issued fraudulent receipts, then created depressions by reducing the supply? Then he was able to confiscate real wealth by seizing collateral put up for loans.

Federal reserve notes are (or were) actually IOU's. A holder of a Federal Reserve note could demand payment from the US Treasury in lawful money of the United States—silver and gold coin. Following the Crash of '29, the demand for redemption of the notes exceeded the supply of silver and gold coin on deposit. The Banking Reform Act of 1933 was in reality a bankruptcy admission by the United States. The Republic of the United States was replaced by the Corporation of the United States. The Fed demanded that the US surrender its gold. Private ownership of gold became a crime punishable by ten years and $10,000.

The Secretary of the Treasury is not a government employee, but an employee of the bankruptcy trustees—the Federal Reserve banks. This is a matter of historical record; check it out for yourself! The United States, in order to stay in business, pledged its collateral—the property and income of its citizens—in exchange for loans to keep the country running. The National Debt is the interest due on these loans.

HIGH TREASON IN HIGH PLACES

In 1910, a German immigrant, Paul Warburg, working with Senator Nelson Aldrich (maternal grandfather of the Rockefeller family), began writing the Federal Reserve Act, yet another effort to create a central bank of issue in the United States. The Act was put before the House on Dececember 23, 1913 (when most members of Congress were home for Christmas), and it was signed into law. The Act placed the Constitutional power of Congress to regulate the US economy into the hands of private banks. After the vote, Congressman Charles Lindbergh told Congress: "This act establishes the most gigantic trust on earth…when the President signs this act, the invisible government by the money power, proven to exist by the Money Trust Investigation, will be legalized…. The new law will create inflation whenever the trusts want inflation." President Woodrow Wilson signed the Federal Reserve Act into law. He was later to observe:

"I am a most unhappy man. I have unwittingly ruined my country. A great industrial nation is controlled by its system of credit. Our system of credit is concentrated. The growth of the nation, therefore, and all our activities are in the hands of a few men. We have come to be one of the worst ruled, one of the most completely controlled and dominated Governments in the civilized world—no longer a Government by free opinion, no longer a Government by conviction

> and the vote of the majority, but a Government by the
> opinion and duress of a small group of dominant men."

A dollar was no longer a unit of measurement. Instead, it
became the thing it was supposed to measure, like turning a
quart into milk. The Federal Reserve system is a private
banking system. It belongs to its stockholders, who are not
the American people. The only stockholders in the Fed are
federally chartered private banks. All the major stockholders in the current Fed can trace their roots to the banking
families of Europe. The first governor of the Fed was Paul
Warburg, now a naturalized US citizen. World War I saw the
creation of the income tax system as a "temporary" measure
to finance the war effort. Now pay attention here—this is a
matter of historical record, as incredible as it may sound!
While Paul Warburg headed the US Federal Reserve, his
brother Max headed the German Secret Service. During
World War I both sides were ably represented by members
of the Warburg family. One would think that, with the Fed
being in New York, that perhaps this apparent conflict of
interest would be picked up by the newspapers. After all,
the *New York Times* ("all the news that's fit to print") built
its reputation on investigative journalism. But the "Gray
Lady" somehow missed the story. Perhaps it was due to the
fact that the *New York Times,* at the time of the First World
War, was owned by Warburg, Kuhn and Loeb! Conspiracy?
I guess that depends on how you define the term. Webster's
defines it as:

> "An agreement, manifesting itself in words or deeds,
> by which two or more persons confederate to do an
> unlawful act, or to use an unlawful act to do an act
> which is lawful; confederacy."

Following Webster's definition, I think a reasonable person might consider the picture, in its totality, as a conspiracy.

BUT WHAT KIND OF CONSPIRACY?

If there is a conspiracy, it is a plan for a benevolent rule by elite. To the elitist, those of his class are uniquely equipped to manage everything by virtue of their disinterested sophistication. The elite aren't somehow evil in nature, they are just arrogant in the extreme. To the European aristocrat, the "educated bourgeoisie" are too dangerous to themselves to be left to themselves. The elitist feels that everything, not just the economy, would be in better hands if only it were all in their hands. This principle has existed through the ages, and if pressed, they will point out that rule by elite was the hallmark of European civilization for 1500 years. This is the backdrop for the so called "money conspiracy"—if the Warburgs, and their peers, don't take control of the economy, the "bourgeoisie" will only ruin it through their ignorance. To that end, another Warburg brother served as commercial attaché in Stockholm, a traditional listening post for warring nations. Warburg partner Sir William Wiseman headed the British Secret Service. Two of Jacob Schiff's brothers financed the German war effort. Another partner, Bernard Baruch, was chairman of the War Industries Board; another key banking insider, Eugene Meyer, financed the war as chairman of the War Finance Corporation. When the war was over, they all met together to sign the Treaty of Versailles. Bernard Baruch headed the War Reparations Board; Max Warburg represented Germany, while Paul Warburg served as advisor to President Wilson. Cozy, isn't it?

THE BANKING DYNASTIES

So where are they today? Through a series of mergers and "acquisitions" the Warburgs, Schiffs, Morgans, etc., control giant stock investment firms. There are few people who have never heard of Morgan–Stanley or one of its affiliates. Swiss Bank Corp. recently "acquired" SG Warburg (now SBC Warburg). In August 1997, SBC Warburg announced its intention to expand its operations more deeply into the US, Japan and Russia. A listing of the major stock brokerage houses of the world read like a "family tree" with a dozen or so names broken up into various combinations. We'll deal with this in greater depth in a later chapter. The same names appear as stockholders in the Federal Reserve, investment "advisors" in stock markets across the world, investment banking houses, the board of governors of the central banks of Europe, and so on. England is the world's largest holder of US debt to this day. The roster of the European Commission reads like a European banker's reunion. The same names can be found in the *Who's Who of American Banking*. Right now, the stock market is breaking records in the US, while Europe "struggles" with monetary union. Meanwhile, the world is being divided by category, into various economic regions like NAFTA, MERCOSUR, ASEAN and PACRIM. All under the watchful eye of the World Trade Organization in Brussels. At the center of it all is Europe, where it has always been. Europe is the birthplace of the global economy. Eventually, everything comes full circle.

HOW THE FED WORKS

Every year, the United States borrowed its operating capital from the Fed at interest. Like the goldsmith of old, the Fed created that money out of nothing by issuing fraudulent receipts (Federal Reserve Notes) for gold it claimed to have in reserve. Except the gold began to disappear. Most of it ended up in the hands of the European banking houses that own the American banks, who are the principle stockholders in the Federal Reserve.

Shortly after the assassination of President Kennedy, a new Federal Reserve note was issued. Some conspirators might point to the fact that President Kennedy ordered, by executive order, the abolition of debit–based money, just before his assassination. Draw any conclusion you wish, but immediately following the assassination, President Johnson canceled the order. As a result, all Federal Reserve notes prior to 1963 promised to "pay to the bearer on demand $XX in lawful United States money." G. Edward Griffin tells this story in his book, *The Creature from Jekyll Island*:

> "Some years ago, a Mr. A. F. Davis mailed a ten–dollar Federal Reserve note to the Treasury Department. In his letter of transmittal, he called attention to the inscription on the bill which said it was redeemable in 'lawful money' and then requested that such money be sent to him. In reply, the Treasury merely sent him two five–dollar bills from a different printing series bearing a similar promise to pay. Mr. Davis responded:
>
> 'Dear Sir:
> Receipt is hereby acknowledged of two $5 United States notes which we interpret from your letter are to be considered lawful money. Are we to infer from this that the Federal Reserve notes are not lawful money? I am enclosing one of the $5 notes which

you sent me. I note that it states on the face, "the United States of America will pay to the bearer on demand five dollars." I am hereby demanding five dollars.'

"One week later, Mr. Davis received the following reply from Acting Treasurer M.E. Slindee:

'Dear Mr. Davis:
Receipt is acknowledged of your letter of December 23rd, transmitting one $5 United States note with a demand for payment of five dollars. You are advised that the term "lawful money" has not been defined in federal legislation.... The term "lawful currency" no longer has such special significance. The $5 United States note received with your letter of December 23rd is returned herewith.'"[2]

"Lawful US money" is silver and gold coin. It was defined, rather specifically, as we have already seen, by the Currency Act of 1792. That promise disappeared in 1964. The bills no longer contained a promise to pay; instead, they themselves claimed to be money. Today the legend reads, "This note is legal tender, for all debts, public and private." Remember, a "dollar" is a measure of a specific weight of silver. Take away the silver, and a dollar is a measure of an unspecified weight of nothing!

Because the US debt is based on money created by the Fed, it cannot be repaid! One cannot pay a debt with a debt. The US owes more money than exists, and every year the negative balance increases. The day is coming when the US will

---

[2] *The Creature from Jekyll Island,* G. Edward Griffin, American Opinion Publishing. p. 136.

be forced—again—to default on its loans. There is very little gold left to surrender. The only remaining collateral is the individual wealth of its citizens. We'll explain how that mechanism works in more detail in Chapter Nine. Eventually, every taxpayer will receive an assessment notice for his share of the debt, currently more than $44,000. How will we pay? With Federal Reserve notes? Hardly. For every taxpayer, there is $44,000 plus worth of Fed notes that do not exist!

At this point, here are a few helpful facts that will bring things into perspective. The United States is $5.5 trillion in debt. That is an amount equal to five times the country's annual Gross Domestic Product. To get a "handle" on how much money millions, billions and trillions really represent, consider the following. One million seconds equals 12 days. One billion seconds is equal to 32 years. And one trillion seconds is equal to 37,000 years! Or, to look at it another way, to pay the national debt at the rate of one dollar per second, it would take something on the order of 185,000 years to break even! The Federal Reserve system, through its ability to create money out of thin air, is in a position to guarantee the federal government will remain subservient to the banking industry in perpetuity. Although Bill Clinton was swept into office as a liberal Democrat, he soon realized the only effective way to govern was to adopt a fiscal policy that President Clinton himself describes as being "an Eisenhower Republican."

Although this sounds like conspirators' theory, it is in reality documented historical fact. The real power remains with the bankers. Remember, eight out of ten of the most powerful men in the world are members of the global economic elite, according to *TIME* Magazine. The other two are politicians.

E N D N O T E

[1]*The Currency Act of 1792*
AN ORDINANCE for the ESTABLISHMENT of the MINT of the UNITED

STATES of AMERICA; and for REGULATING the VALUE and ALLOY of COIN.

THAT a mint be established for the coinage of gold, silver and copper money, agreeably to the resolves of Congress of the 8th August last, under the direction of the following officers, viz.

An Assay Master, whose duty it shall be to receive gold and silver in bullion, or foreign coin, to assay the same; and to give his certificates for the value thereof at the following rates:

For every pound weight troy, of uncoined gold or foreign gold coin, eleven parts fine and one part alloy; two hundred and nine dollars, seven dimes and seven cents, money of the United States, as established by the resolves of Congress of the 8th of August last, and so in proportion to the fine gold contained in any coined or uncoined gold whatsoever.

For every pound weight troy of uncoined silver, or foreign silver coin, eleven parts fine and one part alloy thirteen dollars, seven dimes, seven cents and seven mills, money of the United States, established as aforesaid; and so in proportion to the fine silver contained in any coined or uncoined silver whatsoever.

A Master Coiner, whose duty it shall be to receive from time to time of the assay master, the bullion necessary for coinage; to report to Congress devices and proofs of the proposed pieces of coin, and to procure proper workmen to execute the business of coinage, reporting from time to time to the commissioners of the board of treasury of the United States for approbation, and allowance, the occupation, number and pay of the persons so employed.

A Paymaster, whose duty it shall be to receive, and take charge of the coin made under the direction of the master coiner, and to receipt for the same; to receive and duly enter the certificates for uncoined gold or silver issued by the assay master, and to pay ninety-five hundredths of the amount thereof in gold or silver coin, and five hundredths in the copper coin of the United States.

And be it further ordained, That the certificates to be given by the assay master, to persons who shall lodge gold, or silver in the mint for coinage, shall be on fine bank paper, and expressed in the manner and form following, to wit, ... Mint of the United States, ... 17 ....

I ACKOWLEDGE to have received of A. B. for coinage (here insert the weight) of (insert the species) bullion; for the amount of which, pay to .... or bearer, the sum of .... at ten days sight, agreeably to the custom of the mint. .... C. D. Assay Master.

To F. E. Pay-Master of the Mint of the United States of America.

And be it further ordained, That the salaries of the officers above mentioned shall be per year, payable in quarterly payments; and that they settle their accounts monthly, agreeably to such forms and vouchers as shall be prescribed by the comptroller of the treasury.

And be it further ordained, That the officers mentioned in the within ordinance, shall enter into bonds to the United States, for the faithful execution of the trust respectively reposed in them, in the manner and amount following, to wit,

The assay-master, in the sum of .... Dollars and two sureties, each in the sum of .... Dollars

The master coiner in the sum of .... Dollars and two sureties, each in the sum of .... Dollars

The pay-master in the sum of .... Dollars and two sureties, each in the sum of .... Dollars and that they shall likewise (as well as every other person employed in the mint) take and subscribe the oath of office, established by the resolve of the 14th March 1786.

And be it further ordained, That it shall be the duty of the comptroller of the treasury to report monthly to the commissioners of the treasury of the United States, a statement of the mint accounts, adjusted agreeably to the usual forms; and if on such statement it shall appear, that there has been any neglect, mis-management or abuse of trust, in any of the officers, mentioned in the within ordinance, it shall be the duty of the commissioners of the board of treasury to suspend such officer or officers, and to report thereon specially to the United States in Congress.

And be it further ordained, That the copper coin struck under the authority of the United States, shall be receiveable in all taxes, or payments due to the United States, in the proportion of five dollars for every hundred dollars so paid; but that no other copper coin whatsoever, shall be receivable in any taxes or payments whatsoever to the United States.

And whereas, The great quantities of base copper coin daily imported into, or manufactured within the several states, is become so highly injurious to the interest and commerce of the same, as to require the immediate interposition of the powers vested by the confederation in the United States in Congress, of regulating the value of copper the coin so current as aforesaid.

Be it ordained That no foreign copper coin whatsoever, shall after the .... day of .... be current within the United States: And that no copper coin struck under the authority of a particular state, shall pass at a greater value than one federal dollar for two pounds and one quarter of a pound avoirdupois weight of such copper coin.

And whereas, An uniformity in the punishment of persons found guilty of debasing and counterfeiting the coin of the United States, or knowingly uttering the same, is essential for the prevention of such dangerous offences:

Be it ordained, That if any person or persons shall debase, or counterfeit in any part of the United States, any gold or silver coin struck under the authority of the said states, or shall knowingly utter, or cause to be uttered such debased or counterfeited gold or silver coin, the party or parties so offending shall, if convicted of the same in any court of record established under the authority of the state in which such offence is committed, suffer the pains and penalties of death, without benefit of clergy. And be it further ordained, that if any person or persons, in any part of the United States shall in the manner above mentioned be convicted of melting, or filing, clipping or otherwise impairing the gold or silver coin of the United States; the party or parties so convicted, shall for every such offence be mulcted in a fine of .... dollars, money of the United States, and suffer imprisonment for the space of .... months.

And be it further ordained, That if any person or persons shall in any part of the United States, make coin or counterfeit any of the copper coin of the United States, and be duly convicted thereof in the manner above recited, the party or parties so convicted shall for every such offence forfeit the sum of .... dollars money of the United States, and suffer imprisonment for the space of .... months.

And be it further ordained, That if any person or persons not authorized for such purpose by the master-coiner of the mint of the United States, shall make any stamp, die or mould, in imitation of such as are used in the mint of the United States, or shall convey out of the mint any stamp, die or mould, made or used in the mint of the United States, and shall be thereof duly convicted in the manner above recited, the party or parties so convicted shall for every such offence forfeit the sum of money of the United States, and suffer .... years imprisonment.

And be it further ordained, That the residue of fines imposed by virtue of this ordinance, after defraying the expences incurred on the prosecution for the fame, to the United States, shall accrue to the benefit of the state in which the conviction took place.

All which is most humbly submitted,

SAMUEL OSGOOD,

ARTHUR LEE.

BOARD OF TREASURY, September 20, 1786.

Constitutional Notes:
Section 8 Clause 5 of the US Constitution gives Congress exclusive authority "to coin Money, regulate the Value thereof, and of foreign Coin, and fix the Standard of Weights and Measures."

CHAPTER TWO

THE ULTIMATE HOSTILE TAKEOVER

"If Congress has the right under the Constitution

to issue paper money, it was given them to use themselves,

not to be delegated to individuals or corporations."

ANDREW JACKSON

SETTING THE STAGE

One of the most enigmatic figures in recent history is also one of the most significant. Paul Warburg was so highly respected a financier that he was tapped by Senator Nelson Aldrich to author a study on discounting commercial bills. Aldrich, John D. Rockefeller's father in law, was the chairman of the Senate Finance Committee. Aldrich's committee was charged with developing a central banking scheme for the United States, ostensibly to forestall the financial panics that regularly plagued the US economy at the turn of the century. The United States at that time suffered from periodic liquidity crises, engineered largely by the financial community. Bankers argued that it was due to the rigid nature of the currency supply. In those days, in order to make a loan the banks actually were required to have the money on deposit. A system of pyramiding reserve schemes made it possible for banks to obtain further funds, but they could not actually issue loans until those funds became available. Therefore, the bankers argued, adequate money supplies could not be funneled in time to the industries who needed them the most. To ensure the population got the message, a series of currency shortages were engineered. Since the entire banking system was not yet under a central authority, the "panics' were generally localized in predetermined geographic locations across the States. A large bank, or group of cooperating banks, would restrict credit to farmers and businesses. As a result, industries were often unable to finance inventories or get crops to market. Many went under. Such failures had a ripple effect. Grain rotting in the fields meant a shortage of livestock feed. Higher feed prices forced many livestock producers into bankruptcy. Business failures often weakened other related industries. Ultimately, the pressure was felt on Wall Street, where market prices would plunge; small, weak banks would fail; and the currency supply would be further restricted. The pressure was on. The destruction of the smaller, weaker banking competitors provided two benefits. One is the obvious—fewer independent banks means fewer slices of the pie. Secondly, a small number of big banks is much easier to regulate (control??) than is a larger number of independents. The engineered crises, therefore, provided a payday on several fronts simultaneously. A central banking scheme, argued the bankers that engineered the crises, would eliminate financial panics. All that is needed, went the reasoning, was the ability of bankers to lend more money than they had—at interest. Creating money in this way would enable industry to buy now and pay later when they realized their profits. Of course, for the scheme to work, there would have to be centralized control of the banking system. The problem, argued the proponents of centralized banking, was that there were just too many rugged individualists in the financial community. Wise leadership and absolute control of all banking and monetary policy were necessary to keep these "panics" from repeating themselves.

THE LEADER EMERGES

Early in 1907, Paul Warburg published his official reform plan, entitled "A Plan for a Modified Central Bank." The plan was published in the *New York Times Annual Financial Review*. According to Warburg, the existing system was "evil." He thought the idea of decentralized reserves under the control of regional banking centers was particularly odiferous. Warburg advocated the development of an

American discount market. He argued that the discount market should function on what he called the "real bills" doctrine. Essentially, that doctrine maintained that the money supply should vary according to the short-term legitimate needs of businessmen. Warburg also put forward a plan for a central reserve bank that would hold the reserve funds of member banks. The collective funds could then be made available to member banks suffering from liquidity crises. Remember that a "liquidity crisis" is merely the result of a bank getting "caught" after writing more receipts for gold than were actually on deposit. Back then it was called embezzlement and carried with it a jail term. Warburg's original proposal was more like a form of banker's insurance, a collective pool of cash made available to bail each other out.

WARBURG THE PROPHET

In order to make his argument, Warburg had to overcome what he considered the unreasonable emphasis that Americans put on representative democracy. Opponents of the central banking scheme argued that putting that much control over the lifeblood of the American system—the economy—in the hands of unelected bankers could lead to a kind of banking dictatorship. Their arguments were not without historical precedent. Arguing against the renewing of the Charter for the Rothschild–backed 2nd Bank of the United States, Thomas Jefferson wrote:

> "I believe that banking institutions are more danger-
> ous to our liberties than standing armies. Already
> they have raised up a money aristocracy that has set
> the government at defiance. That issuing power

should be taken from the banks and restored to the government to whom it properly belongs."

To silence his critics, Warburg warned of an impending financial panic that would prove the validity of his plan. The banker's prophecy was fulfilled later that year and is known to history as the Panic of 1907. Once again, credit was refused, the money supply was restricted and businesses failed. Congress was forced to act. The Aldrich–Vreeland Act passed in 1908. Although it didn't go as far as Warburg hoped, it provided for the issuance of emergency currency as a temporary fix. Congress also created the National Monetary Commission to study central banking and other alternatives for monetary and banking reform. Paul Warburg was appointed to sit on this committee, giving him tremendous influence over any subsequent proposals for reform.

THE SHADOW MAN

One of the most interesting things about Paul Warburg is the paucity of information about him. His power and influence were such that the Little Orphan Annie character of the 1930s, Daddy Warbucks, was inspired by the person of Paul Warburg. Yet, despite his immense influence, his wealth and his political connections, he remains all but invisible to the objective historian. One would expect volumes to be written about his life. The Rockefeller family (all of them), J. P. Morgan, Bernard Baruch and other lesser financial figures of the era all have been extensively biographied. But even a brief biography of Paul Warburg is almost impossible to find. A search of *Funk and Wagnall's Encyclopedia* on Paul Warburg returned hits on two footnote sections and one reference. An Internet search of Paul Warburg yielded exactly one entry. Despite the fact that Warburg not only created the Federal Reserve, but also served as its first governor, he is absent from the pages of contemporary American history. Now *that's* power! The late Lady Diana Spencer, Princess of Wales, is often said to have been hounded to her death by photographers. All the power of the British crown couldn't preserve her privacy. Paul Warburg's name is spoken of only peripherally by historians. Those few things we do know about the creator of the American economic system of the 20th century are largely fawning accounts spun by his admirers and financial minions. That's power!

THE MAN WHO WOULD BE KING

Paul Warburg was born in Hamburg, Germany, in 1868. He was the scion of a wealthy German banking family who ensured he received the "best" education. When he was 18, he went straight to London, headquarters of the Rothschild banking empire. Two years later, sufficiently schooled, he returned to Hamburg, where he joined his brothers, Aby and Max, as a partner in the family firm, M. M. Warburg & Co., Hamburg. In 1895, Warburg married Nina Loeb, another offspring of a Rothschild–backed banking dynasty. In 1901, the couple moved to New York. He was immediately offered a partnership in his father–in–law's firm of Kuhn & Loeb, one of Wall Street's most prestigious firms. Soon after entering the world of American–style banking, Warburg began to set in motion a plan for a central bank. Some conspiracy theorists claim Warburg was given his "marching orders" to establish a central bank in the United States while he was apprenticed to the Rothschild group in

London. While there is no direct evidence to establish that as fact, it is interesting to note that the Rothschild group had been attempting to establish a central banking system in the United States since the Revolution. Some may call it "conspiracy." Others may see it as merely coincidence; the facts are what they are. But the possibilities, however they are described, are indeed intriguing.

THE PLAN TAKES SHAPE

After passage of the Aldrich–Vreeland Emergency currency bill, Warburg went on the offensive. The *New York Times* gave him ample space (not surprising, as the *New York Times* belonged to his father–in–law) to expound on the perceived flaws in the bill. Warburg dismissed it as unworkable, saying "no measure that bases currency on a long–term basis like the Aldrich–Vreeland bill (which allowed banks in regional currency associations to use their aggregate bank balances as the basis for issuance of currency) is acceptable."[3]

Or, to translate, "any bill which does not allow banks to create money out of thin air and charge interest for loaning that money, is unacceptable." Warburg argued for an "elastic currency" or, a currency that can be expanded or contracted to meet the needs of the economy. "Expanding" the money supply is really just a euphemism to describe the magician's trick of creating money out of thin air. The authority to either expand or contract that currency would rest with the central banking authority—who would, of course, use that

---

[3] From a paper authorized by Michael Whitehouse for the Federal Reserve Bank of Minneapolis, May 1989.

authority for the public good, whether they agreed with it or not. The fact is, the proposed central bank was to be a private, for–profit banking monopoly.

THE JEKYLL ISLAND CONSPIRACY

Having gained the confidence of Senator Aldrich and the banking establishment, Warburg set out to bring his plan to fruition. Although some might argue that "conspiracy" is too strong a word to describe the Jekyll Island expedition, remember how the word "conspiracy" is defined as you read the following account, taken directly from the Federal Reserve's own literature.

> "One evening in early November 1910, Warburg and a small party of men from New York quietly boarded Sen. Aldrich's private railway car, ostensibly for a trip south to an exclusive hunting club on an island off the coast of Georgia.

> "In addition to Warburg and Aldrich, the others, all highly regarded in the New York banking community, were: Frank Vanderlip, president of National City Bank; Harry P. Davison, a J. P. Morgan partner; Benjamin Strong, vice president of Banker's Trust Co.; and A. Piatt Andrew, former secretary of the National Monetary Commission and now assistant secretary of the Treasury. The real purpose of this historic 'duck hunt' was to formulate a plan for US banking and currency reform that Aldrich could present to Congress.

> "Even Warburg at first questioned the motives of this gathering, not knowing if he was included because the group knew what he preached and was interested in what he had to offer, or if he was to be

involved as a conspirator [note the use of the word 'conspirator' to describe the participants] in order to be muzzled. He soon saw that the Jekyll Island conference was pulled together because, as Warburg later wrote, Aldrich was 'bewildered at all that he had absorbed abroad and he was faced with the difficult task of writing a highly technical bill while being harassed by the daily grind of his parliamentary duties.' One would assume that as an elected Senator from Rhode Island, Aldrich saw that his role as a politician was secondary to his role as developer of a plan to create a private banking monopoly that would profit directly from the people who sent him to office.

"The group was secluded on Jekyll Island for about ten days. All the participants came to the conference with strong views on the subject and did not agree on the exact shape a US central bank should take. Vanderlip noted: 'Of course we knew that what we simply had to have was a more elastic currency through a bank that would hold the reserves of all banks.'

"But there were many other questions that needed to be answered. If it was to be a central bank, how was it to be owned: by the banks, by the government, or jointly? Should there be a number of institutions or only one? Should the rate of interest be the same for the whole nation, or would it be higher in a community that was expanding too fast and lower in another that was lagging? In what open market operations should the bank be engaged?

"Warburg realized that he had not been able to persuade the senator that if a central banking organization was to be created, it had to be a modified scheme based on the European models. In fact, Warburg, 'the best equipped man there in the academic sense,' according to Vanderlip, 'was so intense…and apparently felt a little antagonism towards Aldrich,' so that there were some moments of strain that had to be eased by the others. Aldrich had his mind set on a European–style central bank, 'a model he seemed loath to abandon,' according to Warburg, and the senator strongly believed that the proposed central bank should be kept out of politics [so much for representative government]. Warburg and the others felt that whatever the theoretical justification for such a central bank, American conditions would require some sort of compromise and that concessions should be made considering government influence and representation. Aldrich, yielding somewhat, allowed that the government should be represented on the board of directors [how *nice!*] and have full knowledge of the bank's affairs, but a majority of the directors were to be chosen, directly or indirectly, by the members of the association.

"Warburg also didn't agree with Aldrich's position on note issuance, conditions of membership of state banks and trust companies, or on the need for a uniform discount rate.

"Aldrich insisted, however, that a central bank should maintain a uniform rate of discount throughout the United States. He thought such a measure politically wise because it would refute the charges that other 'great financial centers' would attempt to establish favorable rates for themselves in different regions to the disadvantage of other localities in the country.

"Eventually all of the individuals at the Jekyll Island conference had to modify their views on a central bank plan. Nonetheless, Aldrich got out of the conference just what he intended—a banking scheme that rested upon a consensus of opinion representing the best–informed bankers of this country.

"The banking bill the group brought forth, which came to be known as the 'Aldrich Plan,' called for the establishment of a central bank in Washington, to be named the 'National Reserve Association,' meaning a central reserve organization with an elastic note issue based on gold and commercial paper. The association was to have 15 branches at geographically strategic locations throughout the country. The bank was to serve as fiscal agent for the US government and, by mobilizing the reserves of its member banks, become a lender of last resort to the American banking system. The association as a whole was to serve as a bank of rediscount; that is, it was empowered to discount a second time commercial paper that members of the association had already discounted. By rediscounting, the association could issue [create from thin air] new money that might stay in circulation so long as the paper for which it was issued was not redeemed [remember the goldsmith in Chapter One?].

"No one person was responsible for the final draft bill that was written. It was a record of their composite views. Yet Vanderlip regarded Warburg as having made significant and important contributions to the final result: 'As a philosophical student of banking he was first among us at that time.' Warburg was satisfied that the Aldrich Plan was not a central bank in the European sense. 'It was strictly a bankers' bank with branches under the control of separate directorates having supervision over the rediscount operations with member banks,' he said." [4]

The Fed's own apologists admit the meeting took place in secrecy, under false pretenses, to set up an organization for profit that usurped Congressional authority. A pretense of permitting the government some influence was "granted" by Senator Aldrich, at the insistence of Paul Warburg, to protect the establishment from "charges" they might be motivated by profit. This pretty much fits the definition of conspiracy, as Webster defined it.

THE BIRTH OF THE FEDERAL RESERVE

The Aldrich Plan that emerged from the Jekyll Island meeting was immediately rejected by Congress. The majority accurately viewed it as a plan to usurp Constitutionally granted Congressional authority over the nation's money supply and turn it over to a private banking conglomerate. Another tactic needed to be employed. Paul Warburg rewrote the whole plan, repackaging it as the Federal Reserve Act, and resubmitted it to Congress. To ensure passage, the Act was presented on December 23, 1913, when the majority of

---

[4] From a paper authorized by Michael Whitehouse for the Federal Reserve Bank of Minneapolis, May 1989.

legislators were home for Christmas. It passed without fanfare, and control of the United States monetary policy was quietly transferred from Congress to the banking community represented by the Federal Reserve. Because the Fed was empowered to discount foreign paper (or, contract debt in the name of the people of the United States) it represented the first working model of a globally interdependent economic system. All members of the Federal Reserve System are privately held banks. The principal stockholders include: Rothschild Banks of England and Berlin; Warburg Banks of Hamburg and Amsterdam; Lazard Brothers Banks of Paris; Israel Moses Seiff Banks of Italy; Chase Manhattan Bank of New York; Lehman Brothers of New York; Kuhn, Loeb of New York; and Goldman, Sachs of New York. Rather an interesting assortment when you consider they control the American money supply. Every one of the principle stockholders—all international banks—is in some way indebted and owes allegiance, not to the government of the United States or its people, but rather, to the Rothschild banking interests of London, Paris and Vienna.

A NOTE OF CAUTION

Many people have observed the preponderance of Jewish names included among the principal stockholders of the Federal Reserve and have concluded it is evidence of a "Jewish" conspiracy. That is nonsense, but it is useful propaganda for the anti–Semitic lobby. At its worst, it is a banking conspiracy, totally devoid of any ethnic, racial or religious loyalties. The Jewish people have themselves suffered the greatest losses at the hands of the money trust. In 1939, despite the state–sanctioned rape and pillage of Jewish property, Max Warburg was permitted to emigrate to the United States by the Third Reich, assets intact. Another Warburg brother lived out the war in comfort, openly as a Jew, directly under the nose of the Gestapo. The same money trust that contains so many Jewish names actively financed Hitler's war while simultaneously financing the Allied effort—collecting interest along the way from both sides. Hitler needed the banking establishment's good-will—Jew or Gentile, in order to prosecute his war against the Allies. Seizing the property of Max Warburg or touching the kin of Paul Warburg would have ended Hitler's war effort before it began, and the Nazis knew it. Money is money, and banking is banking, and neither recognizes any allegiances that don't bear compound interest. Six million Jews perished at the hands of the Nazis while the money trust financed I. G. Farben's production of Zyklon B gas. Money trust, yes. Jewish conspiracy? Hardly.

CHAPTER THREE

DYNASTY

"Permit me to issue

and control the money of a nation,

and I care not who makes the laws!"

NATHAN MEYER ROTHSCHILD

In our previous chapters, we've examined the history of money and the role of bankers. In this chapter, we'll undertake the study of banking and corporate influence in America. Each element is critical in obtaining a working understanding of how the global economy functions. To this point, we have only touched on what might be called circumstantial evidence of a "conspiracy" by bankers to influence political decisions by controlling credit and monetary policy. We have seen that, by and large, the origin of much of the capital—and the parent banking firms that control it—is European. In and of itself, that isn't too surprising. After all, the New World was conquered by the Old World—Europe—and everything has to start somewhere. But while the names have become Americanized, the control remains where it has always been. Being able to decipher the agenda provides some insight into what is the actual focus of this book. What does the future hold for America? How will it affect the individual investor and the future of the ordinary American? Is there some way to anticipate trends and allow for some kind of early warning strategy? In this chapter and the next, we will follow the money trail through the decades of the 20th century and see where it leads. It is a little like a road map. Knowing the destination isn't enough. If you can track your journey from your point of origin, by looking where you are, you can get an idea of how much further you need to go. Without all three of these pieces of information, the map itself is useless. The trip itself is long and somewhat complicated by design. After all, if in fact there is a conspiracy, it would need to remain secret to be successful. But nothing happens in a vacuum. To pull off the plan, you need people. So the trick is to hide in plain sight. As we unravel the interlocking directorates and corporate structures that set the global agenda, we'll go behind the scenes into the boardrooms of some of the most trusted and respected companies in America. You might be shocked, maybe even incredulous, but you will be informed. And the old cliché still holds true. *Knowledge is power.* The bankers know that. Now, so will you.

THE DEVELOPING HYDRA

Thomas Jefferson once observed: " **If the American people ever allow private banks to control the issue of currency, first by inflation, then by deflation, the banks and corporations that will grow up around them will deprive the people of all property until their children wake up homeless on the continent their fathers conquered."**

Jefferson's prescient comment was somehow lost to contemporary historians, or at the very least, ignored by the elected officials sent to Washington to protect the interests of the American people. As we have already seen, control of the nation's finances was placed into the hands of the corporate bankers in what can only be described as a bloodless coup d'etat. Although the formal takeover plot came to fruition with the passage of the Federal Reserve Act on December 23, 1913, it only represented the mechanism for governing after total control had been achieved. The opening shots in the battle for control of the lifeblood of America were not actually fired until October 29, 1929.

THE CRASH OF 1929

"It [the Depression] was not accidental.
The international bankers sought to bring about

*a condition of despair here so that they might emerge
as rulers of us all."*

(LOUIS MCFADDEN, CHAIRMAN OF THE HOUSE BANKING COMMITTEE, 1920–1931)

In the six years immediately preceding the Crash, the Fed
increased (or inflated) the money supply by 62%. Market
speculation was encouraged. Once everything was in
place, the bankers who had financed the market speculation issued a 24–hour margin call, precipitating the crash.
The banks were then in the position to loan the government
billions of dollars (at interest) to finance the country out of the
Depression. In early February 1929, the Fed began warning its
stockholders to get out of the market… quietly. The September,
1929 issue of the money magazine, *Review of Reviews,*
expressed its confusion at the mixed signals. It said in an article in that issue:

> "The Federal Reserve statement for August 7, 1929,
> shows that signs of inadequacy for autumn require-
> ments do not exist…the reasons for the Board's
> actions must be sought elsewhere. The public has
> been given only a hint that 'this problem has pre-
> sented difficulties because of certain peculiarities.'
> Every reason which [Federal Reserve] Governor
> Young advanced for lowering the bank rate exists
> now…to do anything to accentuate this is to take the
> responsibility for bringing on a worldwide credit
> deflation."[5]

The prescient nature of the article was exceeded only by the
degree to which it was ignored. Speculation continued,

---

[5] "Review of Reviews," September 1929.

warnings were dismissed, and fortunes were lost. Except for those "in the loop"—like Warburg, Morgan, Rockefeller, and their associates, all major stockholders in the Federal Reserve banking conglomerate.

TRADING WITH THE ENEMY

In 1933, President Roosevelt issued the following Executive Orders; EO6073, EO6102 and EO6111. These Executive Orders were in fact an admission of bankruptcy. Then, on April 5, 1933, President Roosevelt issued Executive Order 6260. The Executive Order proclaimed:

> "All persons are required to deliver, on or before May 1, 1933, all gold coins, gold bullion, and gold certificates now owned by them to a Federal Reserve Bank, branch or agency, or to any member bank of the Federal Reserve system."

The confiscation of private gold was under the authority of a 1917 law, codified as USCA 95a, which allows for exceptional Presidential authority under a "state of emergency." That 1917 law was entitled the "Trading with the Enemy Act of the 65th Congress, October 6, 1917." Who was the enemy? In order for this act to be applicable, the citizens of the United States became the enemy of the new "Corporation of the United States." The Corporation of the United States was the replacement entity for the now bankrupt United States of America! Hard to believe, isn't it? The new Corporation even issued a new flag symbolizing its conquest by the international money cartel. In any courthouse or post office, the flag is on display. We see it in all official photographs of our President. The gold fringe around the official US flag is not decoration. It is the replacement flag. "Old Glory" had no such fringe when adopted. No previous US flag bore such a gold trim. The gold trim represented the country's new owners, the holders of the gold! On June 3, 1933, Congress confirmed the bankruptcy of the United States under House Joint Resolution 192. It was passed during the first Session of the 73rd Congress. In 1968, President Johnson issued another Executive Order that made the takeover complete and absolute. That EO removed the silver backing from our currency. Silver was removed from US coins and a cheaper substitute metal took its place. Without silver, the dollar is valueless, and the United States became utterly insolvent.

"THE TAXMAN COMETH"

"The rank and file are usually much more primitive than we imagine. Propaganda must therefore always be essentially simple and repetitious."

JOSEF GOEBBELS,

NAZI MINISTER OF PROPAGANDA

Prior to 1929, the federal government's size and costs were Constitutionally limited. As a result, it borrowed little and paid very little interest. The Depression overturned the status quo. When the government went officially bankrupt in 1933, it opened the door for taxes to be broadened and increased to finance government borrowing. The "New Deal" entitlement system proposed by President Roosevelt was expensive, far beyond the means of a bankrupt Treasury. Somebody had to pay. The 16th Amendment was a run around the Constitutional prohibition against levying income taxes. To prepare the people, the income tax amendment was widely publicized as the plan to "soak the rich."

The propaganda machine was so powerful that soon, every Congressman in the House was being challenged by his constituency to "have the courage to stand up to the wealthy." As a result of this pressure, Sereno E. Payne of New York introduced the amendment to the House. To his horror, the bill was not immediately struck down as he had hoped. His fellow legislators were also under tremendous pressure to "stand up to the wealthy." Of course, this wasn't the case at all, as we shall see. The income tax provided a mechanism whereby the government could be further indebted to the moneylenders who controlled the Federal Reserve. That mechanism could be broken down into three elements:

1. run up the federal debt;
2. collect the interest on the debt;
3. and, for the money trust itself, to avoid the taxes necessary to pay the interest on that debt.

When, to his astonishment, his own amendment proposal was made it through Congress, Congressman Payne denounced his own proposal from the House floor.

> "As to the general policy of an income tax, I am utterly opposed to it. I believe with Gladstone that it tends to make a nation of liars. I believe it is the most easily concealed of any tax that can be laid, the most difficult of enforcement, and the hardest to collect; that it is, in a word, a tax upon the income of honest men and an exemption, to a greater or lesser extent, of the income of rascals; and so I am opposed to any income tax in time of peace.... I hope that if the Constitution is amended in this way the time will not come when the American people

will ever want to enact an income tax except in time of war."[6]

It is interesting to note that the 16th Amendment was never properly ratified. Two of the 36 states that had allegedly ratified the amendment were California and Kentucky. There is no record of California's vote, and Kentucky voted against it by a vote of 22 to 9. This is in violation of the amendment procedure set down by the Constitution of the United States, Article V.

T. Coleman Andrews, who served as commissioner of the IRS in the 1950s, offered his opinion on the 16th Amendment following his resignation from his post at the head of the agency. In his view:

> "Congress [in implementing the 16th Amendment] went beyond merely enacting an income tax law and repealed Article IV of the Bill of Rights, by empowering the tax collector to do the very things from which that article says we were to be secure. It opened up our homes, our papers and our effects to the prying eyes of government agents and set the stage for searches of our books and vaults and for inquiries into our private affairs whenever the tax men might decide, even though there might not be any justification beyond mere cynical suspicion."[7]

Andrews rightly assessed the Constitutional conflict with the 16th amendment when he observed:

> "It has robbed you and me of the guarantee of privacy and the respect for our property that was given

---

[6] Congressional Record—House, July 12, 1909, p. 4390.

[7] *The Utah Independent,* March 29, 1973.

to us in Article IV of the Bill of Rights. This invasion is absolute and complete as far as the amount of tax that can be assessed is concerned. Please remember that under the 16th Amendment, Congress can take 100% of our income anytime it wants to.... [T]his is downright confiscation and cannot be defended on any other grounds.... [T]he income tax is fulfilling the Marxist prophecy that the surest way to destroy a capitalist society is by steeply graduated taxes on income and heavy levies upon the estates of people when they die."[8]

According to the Grace Commission, a committee appointed by President Reagan to examine the national debt and budget deficit:

"One hundred percent of what is collected is absorbed solely by interest on the Federal Debt and by Federal transfer payments. In other words, all individual income tax revenues are gone before one nickel is spent on the services taxpayers expect from their government."[9]

We'll examine the national debt and what it means to the average American in greater detail in Chapter Nine. For now, it is enough to know that it's big—really big—and it will impact America for generations to come.

Since the passage of the Banking Reform Act of 1933 that lifted the restrictions on government borrowing, there have been more than 195 tax increases. Three quarters of the national budget are now arguably unconstitutional, according

---

[8] *The Utah Independent,* March 29, 1973.

[9] 1984 Grace Commission, Report to the President, p. 4.

to Article 1, Section 8, Clauses 2–18. The unrestricted tax and spend authority of the federal government has proved to be a millstone around the neck of the average American. For the European banking dynasties that have sought control of the American economy since the War of the Revolution, it has been a godsend. The provisions and exclusions that make the American tax code the most complicated in the world have also provided the smoke and mirrors necessary to "Americanize'" what remains of a privately held international banking system in utter control of the US economy.

TIES THAT BIND

To further understand the corporate and banking influence that permeates every facet of American life, it is necessary to construct something of a banking "family tree." The Federal Reserve is largely controlled by its principle stockholders (see Chapter Two). The largest stockholders in the Fed are the Rothschild Banks of London and Berlin. Nathan Meyer Rothschild began developing an American version of his European dynasty by recruiting, training and underwriting international bankers like Paul Warburg. Under Rothschild tutelage, the great banking houses of both Europe and America developed, thrived and intermarried into a kind of financial royalty. There were several branches to this "family" which has grown, as families do, by generation, until it is almost impossible to separate each from the other. The Rothschild banks nurtured and promoted the J. Henry Schroeder banking family. Over the generations, J. Henry Schroeder and Sons begat Paul Warburg, Kuhn, Loeb and Company, who, through a series of strategic intermarriages within the "royal family" saw the creation of some of the largest banking fortunes in America. Through such "American" banking dynasties, the European parent banks have grown in power and influence in this country while still remaining well in the shadows. This particular branch of the "family" today controls voting stock in Fed shareholders such as the National Bank of Commerce of New York, Hanover National Bank and Chase Manhattan Bank, among others. J. Henry Schroeder Trust Company, New York's influence in American politics, includes seeing two of its former directors, John Foster Dulles and Allen Dulles, respectively, occupy the seats of Director of the Central Intelligence Agency and US Secretary of State (under Eisenhower). Schroeder's banking family was instrumental in bringing along a young, globetrotting financier, Herbert Hoover. Hoover, who had lived abroad for most of his life, was tapped as a candidate for President of the United States at a time when his only American address was the offices of J. M. Schroeder Bank of New York. A Berlin branch of the Schroeder bank served as Hitler's personal bankers during the years up to and including World War II. In early 1933, Schroeder Bank was represented by two American lawyers in a meeting with Adolf Hitler. Hitler needed money to finance his army of Brownshirts, and the bank wanted to see the power of labor unions diminished. A deal was cut, the financing was arranged, and the two American lawyers obtained the necessary contracts. Those two lawyers were John Foster Dulles and Allen Dulles. Finances make strange bedfellows.

Other familiar names in the banking and investment industry whose earliest incarnations were born under the Rothschild wing include Brown Brothers Harriman, J. P. Morgan, Morgan–Stanley, Guaranty Trust, Drexel Burnham Lambert, M. M. Warburg and Lehman Brothers. Together, they control the Federal Reserve Bank of New York, National City Bank, Hanover National Bank. You get the idea.

Former chairman of J. Henry Schroeder Bank, Sir Gordon Richardson was appointed in 1973 as governor of the Bank of England, an unabashed Rothschild property for 200 years.

Through a series of interlocking directorates, the corporate and banking influence of the European houses of banking is complete and almost unbelievable. As we have already discussed, this influence is so pervasive that most people will find it stretches the limits of credulity. And that, remember, is their greatest strength. Once again, let's recap to keep on target. The purpose of this book is to give the underlying background that supports the conclusion that the future of the American economic system lies, not in Washington, but where it has always been, in Europe. So stay with me.

THE FIRST FAMILY OF AMERICAN ECONOMICS

The undisputed first family of the US banking royalty is the Rockefeller family. Although the family's net worth would actually put them rather far down on the billionaire's totem pole at something under $4 billion (Bill Gates, for example, is worth ten times that amount), their influence and power far exceed their economic clout. The global financial structure, far from being a secret, is well–known (to those who dig deeply enough) and well–defined. At the top is the Rothschild Group, centered around the Bank of England and its chartered banks. In Central Europe, we find the Swiss banking system, the survivors of the old Vienna–Genoa banking axis. The Swiss banking system is the hub around which all secret and not–so–secret global financial deals revolve.

A CONTEMPORARY EXAMPLE

The US government concluded in an official report in 1997 that Swiss officials deliberately kept gold it knew had been stolen by the Nazis during World War II. The report charged that the Swiss bankers' "indifference to the needs of the victims of the Holocaust and their heirs persisted until the current international pressures came to bear." Or, in plain English, the Swiss bankers conspired to keep stolen money and claim it as their own until they got caught red–handed. The 200–page report also blames the United States and Britain—or, more accurately, American and British bankers for participating in a 50–year long cover–up of the thefts. The report found that a significant percentage of the gold hoarded by the Swiss came directly from the fillings of Jewish concentration camp victims.

CONSPIRACY OF SILENCE

Fifty years after most of the gold was deposited by the Nazis in Swiss banks, an international conspiracy of silence can be laid directly at the feet of the British and American central banks. In fact, some $70 million worth of Nazi gold is stored in vaults at the Federal Reserve Bank in Manhattan and at the Bank of England. The report suggests both banks knew the gold was stolen, but remained silent until the investigation revealed their complicity. The report was compiled by 11 different agencies, including the State, Defense and Treasury Departments, as well as the CIA and the NSA. The *New York Times* called the report "the most comprehensive study yet of the deceit, intransigence and political maneuvering on both sides of the Atlantic that surrounded what has come to be known as the 'Nazi gold' problem."

There is more than just Nazi gold at stake. Swiss bankers continue to exercise control over non–gold assets it held for the Nazis. Those assets are now worth more than $5 billion. The report does not make any recommendations for the return of those assets.

PROMISES, PROMISES

It seems that the Swiss promised after the war to make a full accounting of the gold and other valuables it accepted on deposit by the Nazis during the war. Swiss banking representatives signed what is known to history as the "Washington Agreement" with the Truman administration in 1946. Initially, the US froze Swiss assets until a full accounting was made. The State Department ordered Swiss assets released shortly thereafter. It also blocked any efforts to use sanctions provided for by the Washington Agreement to force the Swiss to live up to its terms.

PROOF IS IN THE PAYMENT

The report also concludes the obvious. Switzerland is the banking capital of the world because Swiss bankers know what they are doing. They knew that the German Reichbank was virtually insolvent before the war began. There could be no question in their minds that the vast sums of money Germany began depositing after the war began were stolen. War, generally speaking, is an expensive enterprise. The sad condition of the German economy was one of the principle reasons for Hitler's rise to power to begin with.

But records show that between 1939 and 1945, the Nazis deposited some 13.5 tons of gold into Swiss accounts in Germany's name. Of that total, the Swiss reluctantly returned less than 25%—and only to Italy, Belgium and the Netherlands.

PLANS WITHIN PLANS

The report singles out the Bank for International Settlements. It was created in 1930 to accept reparations payments from Germany for its actions during the First World War. It was headed during the war by an American banker, Thomas McKittrick. McKittrick was a globalist with strong ties to European banking interests. He is suspected of using the bank's international standing to block American efforts to freeze funds Germany was using to prosecute the war. McKittrick maintained the bank was a neutral entity. He specifically denied any looted gold was stored in the bank's vaults. During the war, the bank's sitting board of governors included British, German, Italian and Japanese officials. The 1997 report suggested the Axis powers had virtually taken over control of the global bank and used it to finance its war effort.

After the war, the US government tried to have the bank dissolved. International pressure from the banking community kept the bank alive in spite of political efforts to close it down. Today, the Bank for International Settlements acts as a global clearing house for major bank transactions around the world.

THE "C" WORD

There are those who dismiss out of hand the existence of an international banking conspiracy. Many simply find it hard to believe. Others are afraid to speak out—especially today, when the mere mention of the word "conspiracy" conjures up images of militia groups, bombers, Oklahoma City and Waco. The fact is, no evidence has ever surfaced to connect an American militia to an act of terrorism. The Constitution provides for the right of states to maintain a "well regulated militia." Try mentioning that in public, if you want to stir up a conversation. In the Oklahoma City bombing "conspiracy" originally blamed on the Michigan militia, the "conspirators" numbered exactly…two. Unless you count those who knew McVeigh's elevator didn't quite go to the top floor. Some of them suspected he was capable of the bombing, but no evidence has come up to suggest anyone actually knew in advance. But it continues in the public mind as a textbook example of what can happen if a person dwells too long on the concept of "conspiracy." Especially a global banking conspiracy.

Regardless of its politically incorrect connotations, the Nazi gold story is prima facie evidence of an international banking conspiracy that would make Nathan Meyer Rothschild blush at its audacity.

JUST KEEP PAYING AND PAYING

Item: the Bank for International Settlements was created to collect war reparations from Germany following World War I. It was the crushing nature of those reparations that historians point to as a principle cause of World War II. Adolf Hitler blamed the terms of the Versailles Agreement that demanded those reparations for his invasion of France in 1940. But Germany continued to pay World War I reparations to France, via the Bank for International Settlements, on time, until April, 1945! Wait just a second. Germany conquered France in 1940. Why would Germany—specifically the Nazis—continue to make payments that it blamed for starting the war to begin with to France, a country that it conquered to teach a lesson for demanding the reparations in the first place? Reparations payments continued to flow from Berlin into Swiss bank vaults until April 12, 1945. Inexplicably, the Swiss rejected that last German deposit of 1.5 tons of gold. For historical context, on April 12, 1945, Adolf Hitler was hiding in his bunker, the Russians were on the outskirts of Berlin, and the war was days away from being over. Nobody has been able to explain why, on the brink of military collapse, that Germany would be worried about continuing to pay for damages caused by the Kaiser a quarter century earlier. Particularly since the payments were going to its current, virtually victorious enemies. That rejected 1.5 tons of gold was all that remained of Germany's treasury at war's end. Apparently hoping to plunder the remaining Nazi hoard, the April 1945 gold shipment was ultimately accepted for deposit by a German branch of the Swiss–owned Bank for International Settlements. To the dismay of the Swiss, the gold was impounded at war's end.

SAME NAMES, OVER AND OVER

The answer to the question why is obvious to any historian. As early as 1933, Hitler met with two representatives of Germany's largest bank—J. M. Schroeder Co. The purpose of the meeting was to obtain financing for his private army of Brownshirts while he set about rebuilding the German war machine. J. M. Schroeder Co. was (and is) a principal stockholder in global central bank schemes, including the United States Federal Reserve. The two J. M. Schroeder officials who met with Hitler to discuss financing his rise to power were American lawyers representing the German bank. They struck a bargain whereby the bank would finance Hitler if Hitler agreed to certain favors in return. The Nazis were to break the backs of Germany's labor movement and pass sweeping legislation giving unprecedented power to business and industry. And Germany was to continue its World War I war reparations schedule to the Bank for International Settlements—of which J. M. Schroeder Co. had a significant interest. As we have already seen, those two American lawyers who negotiated the deal were brothers: John Foster Dulles, a future US Secretary of State, and Allen Dulles, a future director of the CIA.

CONTROLLING THE COLONIES

In the colonies, the Oppenheimer Group, through their control of major Canadian banks like The Royal Bank of Canada and the Bank of Montreal, dictate monetary policy.

The United States banking system is under the control of the Federal Reserve (which is owned by the stockholders who are pretty much defined in the previous paragraph). In the pecking order in the US we find Kuhn, Loeb & Co., Lehman Brothers, and other firms who make up the old Rothschild–US front companies. Far down the list, in terms of dollar values, we find the Rockefellers. No paupers, they control some of the country's largest banks, especially the Chase Manhattan Bank of New York. The Rockefeller family has no significant influence (relatively speaking) over the US economy (Bill Gates or Warren Buffet have more), but the control they exert on the US political system is more than enormous. And most of it is behind the scenes. As we have seen, that is the measure of true power, that ability to remain in the shadows, even when under the brightest lights.

THE ROBBER BARON

John D. Rockefeller was the patriarch of this most influential of families. Old John D. discovered the politics of oil, something we'll deal with in a later chapter. He made his fortune drilling for oil, founded Standard Oil, and dedicated the rest of his life to acquiring everything else he could make a deal for. Somewhere along the line, early in his career, he came to the attention of the Rothschild group in London. He received his early financing for his empire from the National City Bank of Cleveland. NCB Cleveland was identified by Congressional investigators as one of the three principle Rothschild banks operating in the United States at that time. Using his "seed money" from NCB Cleveland, Rockefeller set out to earn his title as the country's premiere robber baron. Old John D. crushed anything, or anyone who got in his way, including competitors, labor unions and attempts at regulatory legislation. Late in his life, he decided to "rehabilitate" himself, according to his biographers, and become a philanthropist. He accomplished that by setting up a series of tax–free "foundations" that ostensibly were dedicated to charity. Today those charities, like the Rockefeller Foundation and the Peabody Foundation, have dedicated their fortunes to promoting globalist causes under the banner of peace.

EVEN CHARITY TURNS A PROFIT

In reality, those same foundations continue to double in size from the tax–free investments they make in causes that serve to strengthen the overall control of the global economy, which makes even more money for the foundations. It also affords incredible political power, power that has been the hallmark of the Rockefeller name since the days of Old John D. The Rockefeller Oil Trust, in its various guises, forms the backbone of the so–called "military industrial complex." The Rockefeller Medical Monopoly has afforded virtual control of the health care industry, while the Rockefeller Foundation has a stranglehold on the religious and educational facets of this nation, through its endowments of Public Broadcasting and specific "nondenominational" religious programming.

In 1911, Judge Kenesaw Landis ordered the breakup of the huge Standard Oil Trust. John D. avoided the taxman by creating four great tax–exempt foundations. They became repositories for his "divested" interests as they made a huge portion of his income non–taxable. They can therefore be passed down through the generations without estate taxes, as the enormous sums they "give" away create great lines of influential men eager to trade favors in exchange for various tax–free "grants." Rockefeller money, Rockefeller men, Rockefeller political influence and Rockefeller advisors contributed to the efforts of Vladimir Lenin (father of the Russian Communist Party), Leon Trotsky, and the Nazi Party. The contributions made directly by the various Rockefeller Foundations, as well as assistance provided by Rockefeller companies, provided Hitler with all the money and material he needed to plunge the world into war. That war made a lot of money for the "military industrial complex" of both sides. When the war was over, and the dust cleared, there were plenty of shattered cities, plenty of shattered lives, and plenty of national IOU's. There were also plenty of people who owed favors to the Rockefeller family. It also rewrote the old rules. In the old days, nations paid big money to be victorious in war. Until war became unthinkable. Now the big profits were in promoting the fear of war and the drive for peace "at all costs." It's that "all costs" part that made the money trust dizzy with anticipation.

All this clout brought one Rockefeller, Nelson Aldrich (named for paternal grandfather Senator Nelson Aldrich, co–architect of the Federal Reserve System), within a heart-beat of the Presidency. Unfortunately, Vice President Rockefeller's heart gave out first, in the amorous embrace of a young TV anchorwoman. (The details were mysteri-ously covered up by the "free" press—owned in large part by the Rockefeller family).

But there were other members of the family more skillful in working behind the scenes. They were considerably more discreet. Chief among them was David Rockefeller.

WAR, PEACE AND PROFIT

In the closing days of World War II, the Allies began to debate the future of the post–war world. The technological and political changes made necessary by the war made all previous rules obsolete. Wars were no longer profitable. With the development of nuclear weapons, there was only one weapon to sell. Unlike conventional weapons, it didn't need to be replaced after use. There was no money to be made in financing the rebuilding of cities. Nuclear war meant no cities to rebuild. Nations would necessarily have to develop some kind of global structure. Isolationism as a political ideology today is an anachronism. For the first time in history, peace is more profitable that war.

THE SOLUTION TO THE PEACE PROBLEM

To this point in history, war has been the ultimate test of a government's viability. If it couldn't successfully meet the challenge, it could not survive. In wartime, civil liberties are suspended as needed. Civil prosperity becomes secondary to the war effort. The solvency of the national treasury takes a back seat to the war effort. As a result, all that is necessary to keep a government deeply in debt is a war, or the threat of war. The greater the threat, or the more destructive the war, the greater the need for debt. Unfortunately, the development of the A–bomb meant the United States, the international banking industry's greatest cash cow, no longer had a credible enemy. No conventionally armed nation would dare challenge the United States after the demonstrations at Hiroshima and Nagasaki. The solution to the problem was to finance a hostile enemy. The international banking cartel had long been a secret patron of the Communist regime. Money was funneled, along with necessary technical secrets, to enable Russia to develop its own nuclear devices. The arms race was on, and the debt ballooned for both countries. Still, the weapons must never be used or the gravy train would grind to a halt.

THE DRIVE FOR PEACE

Representatives of 50 nations met in San Francisco to discuss the development of a supra–national political body. It was organized along similar lines to the defunct League of Nations—but without the built–in flaws that caused the League of Nations to collapse.

The League of Nations was first formally proposed by President Woodrow Wilson as part of his 14–point summary of Allied aims in World War I. That plan formed the basis of the Covenant of the League of Nations, the 26 articles that served as operating rules for the League. The Covenant was formulated as part of the Treaty of Versailles that ended World War I.

Interestingly, although President Wilson developed the plan and was a member of the drafting committee, the United States was never a member. The Senate refused to ratify US membership because it violated Article X of the Constitution. As a result, although at one time or another the League had as many as 63 nations, it had no real authority. Like the UN, it had a security council composed of permanent members, and each permanent member had veto authority. It sponsored global associations like the Permanent Court of International Justice and the International Labor Council. The basic premise of the League of Nations, like the United Nations after it, was that there is safety in numbers—the principle of collective security.

The League had the backing of committed globalists like Wilson, the Rockefeller family, Henry Ford, etc. It enjoyed the backing of powerful international banking families like those who form the power structure of the Federal Reserve. Still, historians dismiss the League of Nations as an idea ahead of its time. As one encyclopedia notes:

> "Never truly effective as a peacekeeping organization, the lasting importance of the League of Nations lies in the fact that it provided the groundwork for the UN. This international alliance, formed after World War II, not only profited by the mistakes of the League of Nations but borrowed much of the organizational machinery of the League."[10]

---

[10] Copyright © 1993 Funk & Wagnall's Corporation.

THE UN "GODFATHERS"

On July 29, 1921, a group of leading international bankers and political figures met to form a Council whose purpose, at least ostensibly, was to advise their respective governments on international affairs.

> "Money for the founding of the CFR came from J. P. Morgan, Bernard Baruch, Otto Kahn, Jacob Schiff, Paul Warburg and John D. Rockefeller, among others. This was the same crowd involved in the founding of the Federal Reserve. The Council's original Board of Directors included Isaiah Bowman, Archibald Coolidge, John W. Davis, Norman H. Davis, Stephen Duggan, Otto Kahn, William Shepherd, Whitney Shepardson and Paul Warburg."[11]

The Council on Foreign Relations (CFR) was (and is) a group of well–heeled, self–appointed "advisors." Their primary agenda is the formation and empowerment of a global government they would control by virtue of the incredible wealth at their disposal.

The CFR, along with its sister agencies—the London–based Royal Institute of International Studies, France's Centre d'Estudes de Politique Etrangre, and Germany's Institut fur Auswartige Politik—are privately funded globalist organizations organized out of the delegates to the Paris Peace Conference after World War I. At the outbreak of World War II, representatives of these organizations offered their services to their respective governments. In the United States, the CFR placed itself (and its money) at the disposal of President Franklin Roosevelt.

---

[11] Kah, Gary, "Enroute to Global Occupation," Huntington House, 1992.

"[The] organization became virtually an agency of the US government when World War II broke out. The Rockefeller Foundation had started and financed certain studies known as 'The War and Peace Studies,' manned largely by associates of the Council; the State Department, in due course took these Studies over, retaining the major personnel which the Council on Foreign Relations had supplied."[12]

The CFR revived the idea of global "collective security" and, together with its sister organizations in other Allied capitals, began advancing the cause for a post–war global body to replace the ineffective League of Nations. Their arguments were persuasive and obviously well–planned in advance. So far in advance, that less than a month after the United States entry into the war; at a conference held in Washington, DC, on January 1, 1942, the 26 governments then at war with the Axis powers declared that they "subscribed to a common program of purposes and principles embodied in the joint declaration…known as the *Atlantic Charter*." The statement embodying this adherence to the charter, called the United Nations Declaration, was later signed by most of the free nations of the world and formed the basis of the UN organization established at San Francisco in April–June 1945.[13]

THE BIRTH OF THE UNITED NATIONS

On April 25, 1945, delegates from 50 nations met in San Francisco for what was officially known as the United Nations Conference on International Organization. Over the

---

[12] Kah, Gary, "Enroute to Global Occupation," Huntington House, 1992.

[13] Copyright © 1993 Funk & Wagnall's Corporation.

next two months, the delegates drafted a 111–article charter that formed the basis for the creation of a United Nations. In what became a typical United Nations tactic, ratification by individual nations became a mere formality. The Charter was approved on June 25, 1945, and signed the next day. The charter was not actually ratified by the peoples of the signatory nations until October 25, 1945. Interestingly, the same provisions of Article X of the Constitution that prevented the United States from joining the League of Nations were apparently no longer an obstacle to the US accepting full UN membership, despite the fact that the basic ideological conflicts with the Constitution remained. Like its predecessor, the United Nations existed solely as a debating society during its first few years of existence.

The world was polarizing: East against West, Arab against Jew, North against South. Prewar European colonial empires began to disintegrate, and suddenly everybody looked to the United Nations. The United Nations looked to its "advisors," the Council on Foreign Relations and the Trilateral Commission.

THE TRILATERAL COMMISSION

David Rockefeller's resumé, according to the official press release of the Trilateral Commission, is as follows:

> David Rockefeller, Jr., is chairman of Rockefeller Financial Services, Inc., and an active participant in the nonprofit arena, especially in the areas of philanthropy, public education, the environment, and the arts.

> Mr. Rockefeller is chairman of Recruiting New Teachers, Inc., an organization dedicated to improving the quality and diversity of the national teacher

work force, and he is a member of the Harvard Overseers' committee on university resources.

Mr. Rockefeller is a trustee and the former chairman of the Rockefeller Brothers Fund and the Asian Cultural Council.

He is an honorary trustee of the Brookings Institution and sits on its education advisory committee, and is a member of the Council on Foreign Relations.

He is a trustee of the National Park Foundation and vice–chairman of the Alaska Conservation Foundation, as well as a founder of the Alaska Fund for the Future, which is supported by residents of the Lower 48 dedicated to preserving both the Alaskan natural environment and its native cultures.

Mr. Rockefeller sits on the board of the Museum of Modern Art, where he also chairs the trustee committee on education.[14]

David Rockefeller carried the original concept of the Council on Foreign Relations one step further. In addition to recruiting the best and brightest politicians, the Trilateralists openly embrace members of the banking establishment and the media. Rockefeller's hegemony over those three spheres of influence—political, financial and educational—make him one of the most influential men this country has ever produced.

Rockefeller's idea for establishing the commission emerged after he had read a book entitled *Between Two Ages* written by an Establishment scholar, Prof. Zbigniew Brzezinski of

---

[14] *The Trilateral Commission Official Biography Server*—WWW.

Columbia University. Brzezinski later served as national security advisor to President Jimmy Carter.

In his book, Brzezinski proposed a vast alliance between North America, Western Europe and Japan. According to Brzezinski, changes in the modern world required it.

"Resist as it might," Brzezinski wrote elsewhere, **"the American system is compelled gradually to accommodate itself to this emerging international context, with the US government called upon to negotiate, to guarantee, and, to some extent, to protect the various arrangements that have been contrived even by private business."**

SUMMARY

To this point, we have made something of a thumbnail sketch of the history of money and how the control of that money translates into unseen and untouchable political power. The power behind the scenes originates, not in the United States, but in the financial centers of Europe. The principal backer of those financial centers is the Rothschild interests in London. Of the three largest foreign holders of US debt, America's number–one creditor is the United Kingdom, via the Bank of England. The purpose of this book is not to advance a conspiracy theory. Either there is a conspiracy, or there is not. Each reader will have to reach his own conclusion on that score. The evidence is what the evidence is. It speaks for itself. But the circle is drawing to a close. As with any circle, it begins and ends at the same place. The global economy was born in Europe. Its trip around the globe is nearly complete, and it will end where it began—in Europe. For the investor, that is information more valuable than Rothschild's advance knowledge of the outcome of the Battle of Waterloo. Now that we have looked at the history, it is time to take a look at contemporary events. From there, the future should be fairly obvious.

• • •

CHAPTER FOUR

DOING THE WASH

"I'm not a crook"

RICHARD MILHOUS NIXON

In order to understand the global economy and the method in which money travels, it's helpful to understand how the underground economy works. As much as $500 billion per year circulates the financial capitals of the planet, untaxed, untraceable and unreported. Much of that money finances quasi–government operations, like the Iran–Contra scandal or the more recent Democratic National Committee campaign finance irregularities that put many of our politicians into office outside of the legal channels of democratic process. Much more goes to finance the drug trade. All of it moves in and out of banks, generally with the willing cooperation of international bankers, using various loopholes in the law. Sometimes the money is transferred outside the law, again with the willing cooperation of some international bankers. Usually the illegal money transfers mean a bigger percentage in fees. The term to describe these illegal funds transfers is money laundering.

MAKING DIRTY MONEY CLEAN

The term "money laundering" is often attributed to a scheme supposedly developed by the Al Capone to hide his ill–gotten gains through the purchase of a chain of unproductive, permanently out–of–service laundrymats. Capone and his men would use the laundrymats to generate bogus income which could be reported as profits when, in fact, the laundrymats were a losing proposition. The "income" reported thus became "clean"; that is, it had an identifiable source not related to organized crime activity. The story isn't true, but the principle is workable. Once legitimized, dirty money could be funneled into the mainstream economy, enabling the gangsters to enjoy the fruits of their labor without raising the suspicion of the authorities. It also provided a ready source of tax–deductible expenses, adding a little icing to the cake. The authorities were never able to prove anything against the murderous mobster Al Capone, despite his reputation. The law won't allow a conviction based on reputation, no matter how vicious that reputation is. And, that same reputation made it virtually impossible to obtain witnesses, even if an honest jury could be impaneled. At the end of the day, the best the prosecution could come up with against Capone was income tax evasion. Proving tax evasion required no victim testimony, no witnesses to be bribed, no jury to be tampered with, no police to be paid off. All that needed to be proved was that the suspect had money that had not been reported as income—in short, a conviction based on lifestyle. Even a crooked jury would have difficulty denying the obvious. Expensive cars, lavish estates and fat bank balances don't fall out of trees, or everybody would have them. Even poor people pay taxes and resent having to do so. Using income tax laws to get a criminal off the street was much easier than using criminal statutes. "Beating the rap" for guys like Capone was generally accomplished by a combination of intimidation, bribes, and that curious respect much of the public felt for high–profile gangsters, especially during the Depression. By using the tax statutes, the government could use one of the oldest tricks in the book—class envy. It's one thing to sell booze. Some might argue that gambling is just a tax on the stupid. Prostitution and drugs are optional vices, and nobody has to patronize these products who doesn't want to. But evading taxes strikes a universal chord. If I have to pay, so should everybody else. The mob recognized the fact that the government had located their Achilles heel. Thus began the gambling operations of Las Vegas, offshore casinos and other legal or quasi–legal, cash–only enterprises. The irony is this. It wasn't the mob that coined the term *money laundering,* despite the fact they are among the best at "doing the wash." Although the money washing scam was already part of standard mob operating procedure, the term itself first surfaced in 1973 in relation to the activities of the President of the United States during the Watergate investigation.

CREEP

There is probably no better object lesson in the mechanics of money laundering than the scandal that gave it its name. The singular dichotomy of American democratic politics is this. Obtaining high office is more a case of being able to raise the purchase price than it is raising the votes. If you have the money, you can buy the votes. The legality lies in just how you buy them. Outright bribery is tacky and therefore illegal. Raising campaign financing, on the other hand, is an art form and therefore legitimate. In 1972, the staff of President Nixon's Committee to Re–Elect the President (CREEP) began assembling the campaign war chest for Nixon's upcoming bid to recapture the Oval Office. Nixon's campaign staff was somewhat hamstrung by an annoying campaign finance law that came into effect on April 7 of that year. That law prohibited anonymous campaign contributions. Many of the Nixon donors preferred to remain in the shadows, especially those large corporations that benefited from a grateful White House. Sweetheart deals based on the dollars slipped into unmarked envelopes may make the business world go round, but declaring those contributions would show just how much payola it takes to make it go round a little faster. Those who can pay don't mind, but those squeezed out had an annoying habit of talking to the newspapers about unfair competition practices.

Declared contributions made some donors less generous, but
the CRP still needed to raise the cash. The CRP had its
sources: Howard Hughes, friends in the dairy industry who
owed Nixon favors in return for services rendered, Florida
banker "Bebe" Rebozo. But the illusion of an independent
White House had to be maintained if Nixon could hope to
recapture the Presidency. The Nixon White House had plenty
of damage–control duty on its plate already, thanks to the war
in Vietnam. The scheme was simple, so simple in fact, that
they got caught. But it proves the point. Money dictates politics, and economic forces are the real power behind the throne.
President Nixon probably believed what he was saying when
he said, "I'm not a crook." He was simply working within the
system as it actually exists. Unfortunately for him, he was
caught holding the bag. The measure of the power of the economic forces behind him is indicated by the fact that the
President of the United States turned out to be nothing more
than a pawn to be sacrificed in the game. The players, the international bankers, and their agents, never saw the light of day.

NO GAME FOR AMATEURS

The CRP launderers got caught in the spin cycle when the
news broke of the Watergate burglary. CRP officials sent five
"plumbers" to bug the Democratic National Headquarters in
an effort to obtain advance campaign strategy from the opposition. They should have sent real burglars. Once the
"plumbers" were arrested, the trail began to lead inexorably to
the White House. It turned out that it was laundered campaign
contributions that financed the whole Watergate operation.
International financier Robert Lee Vesco, under investigation
by John Mitchell's Justice Department, arranged for a cash
donation of $200,000. Howard Hughes dropped $100,000

into the CRP. Several hundred thousand more was contributed, in cash and under the table, by various multinational corporations. Here is a sample trail. American Airlines donated $100,000 but needed to keep it a secret. They had a Lebanese company invoice AA for parts that never existed. AA paid the invoice direct to a Swiss bank through the dummy Lebanese company. The money was then wired to the dummy company's New York bank. There, the Lebanese company's agent withdrew the money and handed it to American Airlines CEO George Spater, who handed it over to Attorney General John Mitchell. Braniff Airlines had its Panama City office pay an invoice to a local company for services rendered. The local company was a front; the money paid was handed over to CRP. To cover the transfer, Braniff sold blank tickets for cash. Ashland Oil funneled money to the campaign through a subsidiary in the Bahamas. The problem was, although the money couldn't be easily traced to the contributors, it couldn't be explained away by the CRP once the investigation was underway. White House counsel John Dean understated the obvious in a private conversation with the President recorded for posterity on one of the infamous Watergate tapes. "People around here are not pros at this sort of thing," he said. "This is the sort of thing Mafia people can do—washing money, getting clean money and things like that. We just don't know about those things because we are not criminals and not used to dealing in that business."[15]

MONEY LAUNDERING AS A CONCEPT

All money laundering schemes, regardless of methodology, have several common features. In principle, there must be

---

[15] *The Laundrymen,* by Jeffrey Robinson, p. 9, Arcade Books, 1996.

an effort to conceal both the ownership and the source of the money. The whole idea is to conceal the paper trail. That's why it is as complicated and expensive as it is. The form in which the money is originally received must be changed. One million dollars in $20 bills in a suitcase is hard to conceal. If it goes into the laundromat in that form, it will come out the other side as a manageable, concealable, yet still negotiable bank account. Lots of money is bulky. A million dollars in $100 bills can make five piles a foot high and would weigh more than 22 pounds—hard to stuff into a wallet, even a big wallet.

The paper trail must be obscured. If the trail can be followed from source to final destination, the whole exercise is pointless. And, this is the most important rule. Constant control over the entire process must be absolute. The launderers know it is dirty money; that's why it's in the wash. If anyone along the way steals it, the owner is hardly in a position to call the police and charge them with embezzlement. Each step must be compartmentalized. That minimizes the investigation necessary if some of the loot comes up missing. While the police can't get involved, the general rule of thumb is this: if you know who stole your money, you can make sure he doesn't steal any more. The mob has some pretty effective methods of ensuring this. So, by the way, does the government. The Watergate scandal is an object lesson in what happens if you let people who know too much say too much.

The criminal with money to launder has a big job in front of him. A drug dealer with $5 million has to figure a way to slip as many as a quarter million pieces of paper into the banking system—unnoticed—and still have his funds available to him at the other end. Bringing it into the system is secret, but if it stays a secret, you can't get it out. That is a bit of a problem.

Small amounts are less difficult. For example, laundering $30,000 could be accomplished by going to 15 banks and buying $2,000 in traveller's checks in each bank. or going to the same number of post offices and buying postal money orders. They can then be deposited in any bank in the world or simply put under the bed until you are ready to spend them.

THE TRACKING SYSTEM

Until the Nixon White House gave us the term *money laundering* in the first place, laundering money, or concealing its source and ownership, wasn't a crime, anywhere in the world. Cash was sacrosanct, your money, and where you got it was nobody's business but your own. The international bankers saw an opportunity to solidify their control of the money supply, and the power it brings, even before the technology to create a cashless society was completely in place. The bankers needed to get the public to appoint them as global economic policemen. The plan sounds like hiring a fox to guard the henhouse, because that is exactly what it is. The trick was to convince the public that it was their idea all along.

A public awareness campaign was necessary. The Watergate scandal was the perfect opportunity. By hyping the dangers of uncontrolled cash, the public would demand some kind of control system and demand a solution that the banking system wanted to see in place anyway. And, along the way, provide a nice profit for the bankers who worked the loopholes. Although there is by definition no way to determine exactly how much dirty money is scrubbed clean and put back into the system, the estimates run between $200 billion and $500 billion per year. That makes converting dirty money into spendable cash the world's third largest business, after oil and foreign exchange. In other words, the three largest and most profitable businesses on earth are not only controlled by banks, but also are the businesses of banks, lock, stock and barrel.

To make the system work, and to create a demand for a money laundering business, legislators passed laws requiring that large cash transactions be reported. These Cash Transaction Reports, or CTR's, generally require a form be filed with the appropriate agency in any transaction of cash in excess of $10,000. Persons entering or leaving a country with sums in excess of that amount must declare the money, its source, and its ultimate destination. The argument is compelling, although flawed. By taking the profit out of criminal activity, you eliminate criminal activity. But, unfortunately, it's a pipe dream. Profit is, after all, the motive for criminal activity. By making the mere possession of large amounts of cash illegal, you simply create yet a new opportunity for profit. Instead of eliminating one type of crime, CTR laws just create a new crime, and new criminals, to add to the existing list. The law was meant for good. But its application did nothing more than create a new way to profit from criminal activity while adding one more way to cheat the taxman out of his cut. The banks, however, still get their piece of the pie, and the CTR's merely made that piece so much bigger.

And make no mistake, crime is a big, big piece of the pie. For example, more money changes hands annually for illicit drugs, on a global scale, than it does for food. Think about that for a minute. One could feed the world with the money spent on drugs every year!

CASE IN POINT

The United States Customs Service cracked a money laundering operation in May, 1998. The Treasury Department, in a statement, called it "the culmination of the largest, most comprehensive drug money–laundering case in the history of US law enforcement." How big? More than $35 million was seized outright. Another $122 million was seized from bank accounts in the US and abroad. The money launderers were good. Really good. And of course, they should be. Almost all of those arrested were bankers. Officials from 12 of Mexico's 19 largest banks have already been indicted. One indictment also charges three Mexican banks: Confia, Bancomer and Banca Serfin. Banca Confia is a wholly owned property of Citibank Corporation. The money was collected from couriers for the cartels and deposited in bank accounts in Los Angeles. The money was then transferred to Mexican bank accounts where, the DOJ says, the bankers knew the money was from drug sales. Money transfers by wire between banks, even when they cross borders, are not subject to any of the tight regulations that govern other cash transactions.

All told, 22 Mexican banking officials from 12 banks were arrested in California and Nevada on money–laundering charges. The Mexican bankers who were arrested had planned on a much more celebratory weekend. Undercover agents had used several ruses to lure them to this country. Some had arrived in San Diego, where they had thought that they would be attending a banking conference on money laundering. Others, with whom undercover agents had participated in money laundering activity, were told to come to a purported casino opening in Mesquite, Nevada, where, they were told, their drug cash would be welcomed.

PASSING THE BUCK

Money moves around the planet in breathtaking amounts. Every day, there are more than $1 trillion worth of wire transfers. In today's economy, we hear figures like billion or trillion so often they really don't make much of a picture. A million dollars in $20 bills (most of us are familiar with $20 bills) makes a stack 25 feet high and weighs 110 pounds. The $500 billion represented by the money laundering industry could be represented this way. In $20 bills, it would be roughly 2,368 miles high! It would weigh 27,500 tons! This is not spare change! Let's return to the example we used in Chapter One for clarification. A million seconds is 23 days. A billion seconds is 32 years! And a trillion seconds is 37,000 years! Million, billion and trillion sort of sound alike, but that's where the similarity ends. The banking system gets a piece of every transaction. With the power that the control of such enormous wealth provides, laws can be manipulated to the degree that, no matter the intention, they benefit the banking system as effectively as if they were passed in the banking system's boardroom.

BANKERS WITH BENT NOSES

In the United States, the banker's police force goes by the name of FINCEN, an acronym for the Financial Crimes Enforcement Network. FINCEN is a government institution with its headquarters in Vienna, Virginia, but in the final analysis, it works for the international banking community, even though it doesn't really know it. Through its interlocking sister agencies in the major financial capitals of the world, FINCEN is a sort of banker's Interpol. It relies on the cooperation of international banks to track money launderers and the criminal activity that drives the dollars underground in the first place. That's what makes it a banker's Interpol. When banks launder money, they get a cut off the top. On the other hand, private launderers skim off the cream, and all the banks get are the usual transaction fees…which isn't entirely bad, given the amount of money that is circulated annually. By cooperating with FINCEN, the international banks are able to eliminate competition at will. Provided they throw the governments an occasional dirty bank or two, they are usually able to keep the most profitable deals for themselves. But there is a catch. In order to run things from behind the scenes, they have to assume the risk that once in a while, they might get burned. Such was the case in the BCCI scandal.

BCCI AND THE LONDON CONNECTION

The scandal surrounding the fall of the Bank of Credit and Commerce International was a complicated web of fraud and payola, shell games, dummy corporations, forgeries and conspiracies to hide billions in drug money and other criminal proceeds. The principals read like a "Who's Who" of American government and international business leaders. Names like Robert Altman, Clark Clifford, George Bush Jr., Jimmy Carter, Bert Lance, Henry Kissinger, Senator Orrin Hatch and CIA chief William Casey. Some of these were convicted of various crimes. Prosecutors were unable to obtain indictments on many more. But the scandal reached deep into the hallowed halls of US government and beyond. The tainted money handled by BCCI (sometimes called the Bank of Criminals and Crooks International) went around the globe many times, stopping only briefly at places like the Bank of England, the Vatican, or the secret banking world of Liechtenstein or Switzerland. When the money stopped moving, many honest depositors found themselves holding worthless scraps of paper that represented their life savings. As chief prosecutor Robert Morganthau, of the Manhattan District Attorney's office described it,

> "When the pattern of bribery is so established and so subtle that it cannot be proved in a court of law, then it is almost impossible for a democracy to function."[16]

Another lawyer, Chief of Investigations John Moscow, said in the same article;

> "To put this into the largest possible context, BCCI is a case study in the power of drug and oil money. It all comes together in this bank. The amount of bribery is almost unprecedented."[17]

The participants and principles in the case cut clearly across lines of political allegiance, corporate ethics, banking scruples and public trust to demonstrate how easily money creates power, power corrupts, and absolute power corrupts absolutely. Many of the banks involved directly in BCCI's money laundering scheme are principals in the Federal Reserve. For example, an affidavit entered into a US court

---

[16] "How They Broke the Bank" by Marie Brenner, V*anity Fair,* April, 1992, p. 170.

[17] *ibid.*

revealed that in 1978, the Bank of America held a 30 percent share of BCCI's stock. BCCI enjoyed the full protection of the Bank of England for 15 years. England's
Parliament authorizes and oversees all banking activities in
the United Kingdom. Only a financial institution that has
been authorized, following rigorous auditing and close
scrutiny, is even allowed to use the term "bank" as part of
its name. BCCI avoided this attention by doing business as
a Licensed Deposit Taker. It seems a fine distinction, but it
actually means a great deal. Licensed Deposit Takers are little more than check cashing outlets or banking substations.
Their ability to conduct full banking services is extremely
limited, and so is their oversight by overworked government auditors. BCCI, merely by its name, was in violation
of British banking laws. The Bank of England, America's
largest creditor and flagship of the Rothschild empire, knew
as early as 1980 that BCCI was dirty. In 1985, the Bank of
England was informed by letter of massive fraud at BCCI,
but took no action. To the contrary, BCCI enjoyed a close
relationship with Britain's central bank, in addition to most
of the central banks of Europe and the Federal Reserve
Bank of the United States. Headed by a Arab financier
named Agha Hassan Abedi, BCCI was financed from its
birth by Sheikh Zayed Bin Sultan Al–Nahayani, ruler of
Abu Dhabi. Al–Nahayani and his associates ponied up some
$2.5 million to start the bank. Much of that money came
from the proceeds of loans backed by the Bank of England.
BCCI's approach to banking was novel, to say the least.
With almost no capital (by international banking standards)
it created its own working capital by borrowing from itself.
It circulated drug money using the tried-and-true formula of
taking in dirty money on one end and sending it out the

other end, clean and pressed, in the forms of "proceeds" from loans, taking a cut both ways, of course. In order to accomplish this feat without any actual money of its own, on such a gigantic scale, took plenty of political clout and a willingness on the part of the international banks to look the other way. All of which cost money. When the scheme began to unravel, the shortfall was, in fact, the money paid out in bribes that never existed in the first place. The best estimates exceed $10 billion.

Interestingly—or perhaps more to the point—the international banks managed to keep their hands clean through the whole affair. Only minor functionaries, like Clark Clifford, who played a role in every administration from Truman to Carter, and former White House budget director Bert Lance, ever actually got caught in the spin cycle. The victims got burned, the middle men got caught, and the principal beneficiaries got even wealthier. There must be a lesson in this somewhere. One thing for sure. It denies the old cliché "crime doesn't pay." It pays very well indeed.

CHAPTER FIVE

THE POLITICS OF WAR

"The Arabs can lose

and return to fight another day.

Israel can only lose once."

GOLDA MEIR, ISRAELI PRIME MINISTER, JUNE 1967

THE MIDDLE EAST CONFLICT

We've already touched briefly on the way in which the financial community can reap huge profits from financing wars. We've seen a paradigm shift on the part of global planners to move from a war–based profit scheme to one of turning a buck by promoting "peaceful coexistence"— based in part on selling enough weapons to each side in a conflict to maintain the balance of power. The development of nuclear weapons makes war unthinkable, even for bankers, unless it can be contained sufficiently to leave enough pieces to finance rebuilding efforts. The Middle East is an arms dealer's gold mine, provided nuclear weapons can be kept out of the equation. Europe is far too close to the Middle Eastern theater of operations to risk nuclear confrontation. Much more potential profit is jeopardized by the specter of creating radioactive oil fields than is represented by financing and promotion of regional war. But the pot must be stirred to keep the ingredients from burning, and the necessary spices must be added at just the right moment to keep the recipe from becoming spoiled.

DOLLARS AND SENSE

One of the most critical components of the Arab Israeli peace process can be measured in dollars and cents. The Arab countries surrounding Israel are thunderstruck at the economic miracle that modern Israel represents. They look across their own dry, barren lands at the lush orchards and fertile fields of Israel with awe and wonder. Five times the Arabs have launched concerted efforts to seize the land by force of arms. Five times they failed. Each effort cost the Arabs dearly. Although Israel was outnumbered each time, and although Israeli casualties were proportionately many times higher, Israel emerged from each war stronger, healthier and with a more vibrant economy than before. And after each attempt, the Arabs were that much poorer, the refugee camps that much more crowded, and the outlook for the future that much more dismal.

ORIGIN OF THE PEACE PROCESS

It is for that reason, more than any other, that the Arabs have been willing to at least sit down at the peace table and talk with the Israelis.

The PLO, more than any other group of Arabs, remained militantly opposed to opening any kind of dialogue with Israel. Egypt made peace in 1977, having suffered a crushing defeat at the hands of the IDF in 1973. Jordan could not actually make peace with Israel without suffering politically at the hands of the PLO. But King Hussein is nothing if not pragmatic. Although technically remaining in a state of war with Israel, Jordan and Israel maintained a cordial "back door" diplomatic policy for two decades. But the PLO hatred of Israel remained white–hot. So deep was this hatred that Yasser Arafat was willing to risk it all to support Saddam Hussein in the Gulf War simply because Iraq was willing to launch its Scuds in the direction of their enemy.

Arafat's gamble failed. Saudi Arabia and Kuwait, furious at Arafat's betrayal, cut off all aid to the PLO. Since the PLO received 98% of its funding from these two sources, by betraying them, Arafat destroyed the PLO's economic foundation. Broke and friendless, Arafat came reluctantly to the peace table. It was money, not love, that formed the bedrock upon which the illusion of peace in the Middle East is being built.

But that bedrock is beginning to crack. The MENA conference in Cairo in 1997 caused many of the Arab nations to re–think their strategies where Israel is concerned. The conference was supposedly convened to improve economic relations between the two sides. At some point between planning the conference and the summit itself, the worm turned.

What the MENA conference actually did was give voice to an Arab economic lobby that opposes integrating Israel into the Arab economic picture. Surprisingly, the voices raised most loudly in opposition came from the nations who were believed to have the most to gain. At MENA, Egypt's Hosni Mubarak led the anti–Israeli cheerleading squad. Egypt has embarked on a policy aimed at isolating Israel and moved away from its previous position that peace with Israel is crucial to any new regional economic formula.

The Israeli delegation to the conference was headed by David Levy. Levy was, at that time, Israel's Foreign Minister. Levy was not even permitted to address the opening session. Arab summit leaders were so openly contemptuous that Levy boycotted the remainder of the sessions. Israeli businessmen hoping to come away with new joint Arab–Israeli ventures returned empty handed.

The Arabs seem intent on resuming hostilities with Israel on all fronts, including (or especially) the economic front. Six months ago, Arab–Israeli joint economic ventures forced both parties into commitments that made a lasting peace seem inevitable. Even if they hated each other, the intertwining of their economies would make war impossible. After all, you can't make war with yourself. Defeating Israel militarily would be tantamount to defeating yourself. You can't eat dirt—even Israeli dirt.

DRUMS OF WAR

That is what made recent troop movements in Syria and Iraq so puzzling. Syria couldn't hope to defeat Israel without Egypt's support in the south. Iraq would have to cross Jordan to participate in any attack. Both Egypt and Jordan are formally at peace with Israel. Both countries have significant economic investments at risk. And Yasser Arafat's willingness to abandon Saudi Arabia and Kuwait during the Gulf War all but closed the door to any hope of an Arab unified response. It didn't make much sense. All that is changing. The Arabs are disentangling themselves from alliances and potential alliances that might get in their way in the event of another Arab–Israeli war.

THE GROWING EUROPEAN–ARAB CONNECTION

At the time of this writing, Arafat is busily building bridges with Europe. French President Jacques Chirac toured the Middle East in October on a "fact finding" tour that led him to Jerusalem. There he compared the plight of the Palestinians to the Diaspora and officially supported the creation of a Palestinian State with Jerusalem as its capital. Arafat engineered a free–trade agreement between the PA and Europe that all but grants it official status as a state. A Jordanian newspaper, the *Business Chronicle,* smugly evaluated the new Middle Eastern balance of economic power in the light of the developing European–Arab economic alliances: "So, it would be nice to see who needs who in the new era of peace and prosperity, bearing in mind that the new international arena has vastly changed since the 1970s and 1980s."

Israel is facing hard times. The United States is beginning to reexamine the aid package that forms the backbone of the Israeli economy. The United Nations is once again considering sanctions against the tiny Jewish State, calling Israel a "culture based on sadism." Israel's most effective bargaining chip—its economic power—is beginning to erode.

Arab countries that appeared to be on the verge of normalizing relations with Israel are backing off. Morocco has said it has no further interest in strengthening economic ties with Israel until it makes peace with the PLO on the PLO's terms. Dubai has said basically the same thing. Qatar has frozen further cooperation with Israel. Even Saudi Arabia has forgotten the knife Arafat plunged into its back in 1991. It told the MENA conference there would be no economic cooperation with Israel unless Israel reverses itself on its policy regarding the Palestinians.

The Arabs at the MENA conference wondered if they had over–estimated Israel's economic clout in the region. Israel's Gross Domestic Product is $53 billion. Compared to Saudi Arabia's $92 billion and Turkey's $95 billion, Israel's GDP is not that impressive. And Israel's most implacable enemy, Iran, has a GDP of $139 billion. In terms of dollars, Iran alone outnumbers Israel three to one.

Israel's ratio of economic growth doesn't seem so impressive at 3.2%, either. Egypt's growth rate is 4.4%, Oman is 8.8% and Morocco is growing at the rate of 5.5% per year.

Peace would further erode Israel's financial muscle. Currently, some 40% of Israeli industry is focused in the military sector. In a world without enemies, Israel would see its industrial output cut nearly in half.

THE BANKER'S WAR

The Arabs are beginning to catch on to the realities of war in the '90s. Wars are still fought using conventional weapons—but they are won by bankers. The United States defeated Iraq militarily. The Gulf War resulted in one of the most decisive military victories in history. But Saddam is still in Baghdad. To the Arabs, that is a victory. George Bush was toppled by the 19% margin Ross Perot was able to divert using his billions in the 1992 election. To the Arabs, that is defeat. In the Middle East, wars are fought between leaders. Whoever is still standing at the end is the winner. In the Arab view, George Bush was defeated by a bank balance. The Arabs are gambling that same principle will apply against Israel's government. So is Europe.

THE ROOTS OF CONFLICT

As we discussed elsewhere, war is no longer a friend to the banking establishment. There is far greater profit to be made by maintaining a balance of power. One of the most poorly guarded secrets on earth is the fact that Israel is a nuclear power—the only nuclear power in the Middle East. (At the time of this writing, Iran is catching up fast) The Arab–Israeli conflict is a religious conflict; the international financial community has no interest in a military defeat of Israel for any particular reason except the Arabs want them pushed back into the Mediterranean Sea. At issue is the city of Jerusalem, and in particular, the Temple Mount, or al Aqsa Mosque, depending on which side of the religious equation you sit. To Israel, the Temple Mount, which sits squarely in the center of the Old City of Jerusalem, is their holiest site. According to the Hebrew Bible, Jerusalem is

Israel's eternal capital. A 3,000–year–old passage in the Book of Psalms expresses the depth of Israeli emotion over the city.

> "If I forget thee, O Jerusalem, let my right hand forget her cunning. If I do not remember thee, let my tongue cleave to the roof of my mouth; if I prefer not Jerusalem above my chief joy" (Psalm 137:5,6).

On the other hand, the Koran (the Islamic sacred writings) identifies Jerusalem, in particular, the area known as the Temple Mount, as the place where the Prophet Muhammad ascended into heaven on a winged steed.

Therefore, the place is sacred to both Arab and Jew, and each side wants to possess it exclusively. If the potential for war can be controlled, there is much money to be made financing the arms trade. While the financiers have no particular religious preference in the conflict itself, religion has always been very profitable as a catalyst for extending credit. But things have to handled delicately. The Israelis are a financial capital, but finance is only money, and money can be invented as needed, as we have already seen. The Arabs, on the other hand, have oil. Radioactive oil has no value, and oil is the world's largest business. If Europe is to take a side in the conflict, it will not be based on ideology—it will be based on profit and loss. Any Israeli nuclear threat must therefore be neutralized.

LEGACY OF THE GULF WAR

When Saddam Hussein invaded Kuwait in 1990, the world mobilized against him. The reason was the threat Iraq posed to the vast Kuwaiti and Saudi oil fields. As we have already observed, "he who has the gold makes the rules." Nobody, especially the international financial community, wanted to see an unstable despot like Saddam Hussein dictating global policy. Saddam's values are unstable. He isn't motivated totally by profit, so he would be difficult, if not impossible, to control. His "scorched earth" policy, demonstrated by the deliberate firing of the Kuwaiti oil fields, proved he could only be an asset to the international financial community in a supporting role. Therefore, although he was decisively defeated on the battlefield, he was allowed to remain in power in a considerably diminished Iraq.

WEAPONS OF PEACE

The sanctions have been in effect since the end of the Gulf War in 1991. One of the terms of the Gulf War cease fire was that Iraq would destroy all weapons of mass destruction. That would include chemical weapons and nerve gas. Iraq claimed at the time it had only a "few grams" of a nerve gas called VX gas. VX gas is so toxic that a single drop on the skin can kill a man in seconds. And Iraq has almost 9,000 pounds of it hidden away, according to UN investigators. Publicly the Iraqis deny having any gas or violating any other part of the cease–fire agreement. UN Commissioner Rolf Ekeus confronted the Iraqis with hard evidence and claims the Iraqis admitted to manufacturing the gas. The UN says Iraq also claims it destroyed the gas on its own, without UN verification. Iraq's weapons of mass destruction are real. But they are carefully controlled, like a hand grenade with the pin firmly locked in place. The threat is all that is necessary, as we shall see as we go on.

THE SYRIAN THREAT

Syria also has a credible chemical weapons program. Syrian

chemical plants near Aleppo and Damascus are churning out toxic chemical and biological weapons at an incredible rate. Most of the raw materials are supplied by companies in both France and Germany. Syria's Hafez al–Assad is a pragmatic enough leader to recognize where the real power comes from. Therefore, he can be trusted with the trump cards necessary to neutralize the Israel nuclear threat. Working through the former Soviet Union and Red China, Syria has been able to obtain enough mobile missile launchers to launch a barrage, if necessary. Syria has enough Russian S–300 missiles, Chinese and Korean Nodong 1 missiles and advanced missile technology to enable it to strike anywhere in Israel. These missiles are capable of carrying chemical, biological, or even nuclear payloads. Thirty missiles armed with VX gas warheads and poised for launch against Israel are a sufficient deterrent to an Israeli nuclear attack—or, at least, that is the plan. As efficient as the Israeli Defense Forces are, VX warheads can't be stopped using Patriot missiles or other technologies. Detonating a warhead filled with poison gas would merely release the gas, and that's the object of the exercise to begin with.

EGYPT'S MILITARY BUILDUP

The following is a breakdown, according to the US Arms Control and Disarmament Agency, Russia's Federal Intelligence Service and other intelligence sources, of Egypt's extensive development of weapons of mass destruction. In a 1993 report, "Proliferation of Weapons of Mass Destruction," the Russians note that while there is "no special program of military–applied research in the nuclear sphere," there have been some developments of note.

Among them:

- Egypt agreed to purchase a 22–MW research reactor from Argentina during 1992.

- Egypt is paying India to upgrade a 30–year–old Soviet research reactor from 2–MW to 5–MW.

- Egypt has contracted with Russia to supply a cyclotron accelerator, which would be helpful in exploring uranium enrichment technologies.

- Egypt has begun building a facility at its Inshas research center, which the Russians note: "in its design features and engineering protection could in the future be used to obtain weapons–grade plutonium from the uranium irradiated in the research reactors."

CHEMICAL WEAPONS

The Egyptians are also interested in chemical weapons. Specifically, the FIS document notes: "Techniques of the production of nerve–paralyzing and blister–producing toxic agents have been assimilated." Furthermore, the FIS said: "There is information to the effect that Egypt is displaying interest in purchases overseas of warheads intended for filling with liquid chemical warfare agents. The stockpiles of toxic substances available at this time are insufficient for broad–based operations, but the industrial potential would permit the development of the additional production in a relatively short time."

BIOLOGICAL WEAPONS

The Egyptians also have a biological weapons program,

according to recent statements by the Russian FIS and the CIA and the US arms control agency. **"At the start of the 1970s,"** the FIS said, **"President Sadat confirmed this, announcing the presence in Egypt of a stockpile of biological agents stored in refrigerating plants. Toxins of varying nature are being studied and techniques for their production and refinement are being developed at the present time in a [unnamed] national research center."**

In response to a question during a US Senate hearing in 1993, CIA Director R. James Woolsey confirmed that Egypt is counted as a nation with biological weapons capability. In the three annual reports to the Senate Foreign Relations Committee since 1995, ACDA has used the same language to assess the Egyptian program: **"The United States believes that Egypt had developed biological agents by 1972."**[18]

IRAN—THE JOKER IN THE DECK

According to a report in the *Washington Times,* both Russia and China are assisting Iran in the development of ballistic missiles. The *Washington Post* article quotes unnamed senior Pentagon sources. In September, 1997 Israeli television news reported that Israeli intelligence officials predict that Iran will be ready on the missile front in under three years.

Iran is the joker in the deck—virtually impossible to control, but necessary to maintain a balance of power in the Middle East. Iran's Islamic government needs to maintain a

---

[18] Source: US Arms Control and Disarmament Agency, 320 21st St. N.W., Washington, DC 20451.

balance of power at home in order to stay in power. January 1997 marked the 18th anniversary of the Islamic revolution that rewrote the political rules of engagement in the Middle East forever. Until the fall of the Shah of Iran, Iran was America's eyes and ears in the Middle East. Today, Iran represents the biggest threat to peace in the entire region.

Washington has spent most of the past two decades trying to isolate Iran as an outlaw state. They haven't been nearly as successful as the spin doctors tell us, however. Iran simply turned its attention to the east where it has plenty of friends who are more than happy to trade Iran's oil dollars for hard weaponry. As fast as tension is building in the Middle East, Iran's arsenal is being built even faster. Beijing has sold Tehran 10 Hegu–class fast–attack missile craft. Each is armed with C–802 anti ship cruise missiles. Those missiles can carry a 500–pound warhead to targets 70 miles away. Iran has built up surface–to–surface missile batteries along its coast and stationed missiles on several Gulf islands. Its arsenal includes some 300 CSSC–2 Chinese Silkworm missiles and 100 CSSC–3 Seersucker missiles. Moscow has been only too happy to trade surplus weapons for hard currency; the Iranian navy now boasts three Kilo class Russian–made submarines. Iran has an extensive inventory of SCUD missiles. North Korea is expected to bolster that inventory with long–range Nodong missiles that will put the whole Middle East in the sights of Iranian gunners.

There are rumors that Russia is also supplying Iran with nuclear technology. That is expected to give Iran long–range nuclear weapons capability within the near future. But there are lots of other countries eager to fill Iran's military wish list as well. India is working with Iranian intelligence in its cold war with Pakistan. Both India and Pakistan are nuclear countries. Pakistan is predominantly Muslim. If an Iranian–Indian alliance becomes too threatening, Pakistan can make Tehran an offer too good to refuse. If Pakistan were to offer nuclear technology, Iran could simply switch sides on religious grounds.

Basically, the Iranian system is a theocracy—that is, a state run entirely according to religious doctrines. That gives it considerable power over its citizens. There is no enemy more dangerous than the one who believes he has God on his side. But even religious fundamentalists have to eat. To keep Iran's power base intact, and to keep them at bay, the international financial community is careful to keep the Iranian economy humming along smoothly, despite the fact that their chief manufacturing export is still Persian rugs. Germany and France are not shy about doing business with the Iranians, either. German and French companies have been involved with Iran for years in both nuclear and chemical projects that could easily be converted to military use.

Iran's economic report card is much better than one would expect, if US sanctions were having any effect. During 1997 Iran's economy grew 4%, up from 3.5% the year before. And inflation is dropping. Economists predict it will bottom out close to 20% this year, down from 50% last year.

The United States is considering taking military action against Iran—if it can make a case that Iran was behind the 1996 bombing of the US military barracks in Dharan that killed 19 servicemen. The Ayatollah Khomeini issued a warning to Saudi Arabia if such an attack occurs. He said;

"If any of these foreigners in the Persian Gulf makes

one miscalculated move that could lead to instability, the first country that will burn will be the one that invited these foreigners here in the first place."[19]

The Middle East is ripe for an explosion of violence. Europe, China and Russia are taking steps to hedge their bets in advance. Any explosion will be directed toward the United States and its allies.

NEUTRALIZING AMERICA

A number of miniature Russian nuclear devices had mysteriously disappeared from the Russian nuclear inventory. Russian General Alexander Lebed let it be known those nukes could be in the hands of terrorist groups. Those nukes are small enough to fit inside an ordinary suitcase. Russian professor Aleksy Yablokov told a legislative commission those nukes are real. There are also far more of these weapons on the loose than we had originally believed. In a recent television interview, Yablokov said he had actually talked to some of the developers of these weapons. More than that, he says that the KGB constructed 132 of them. Eighty–four are missing. According to Yablokov, the weapons were developed for one purpose. The KGB developed them to be exploded in strategically located American cities, in his words, "at the right moment." The weapons are designed without fail–safe codes. That means they can be detonated without Presidential approval. By making it public that the weapons are outside Russian control, Russia also has plausible deniability.

If the Russians don't have them, the US can't very well

---

[19] *Countdown Magazine.*

threaten retaliation if they are detonated by a Middle East terrorist group. As we already pointed out, there is a definite effort to reduce American influence in global politics. Nowhere is that more important than in the Middle East. The Arabs are working to develop offensive missile systems that can deliver chemical weapons payloads within Israel. In the event of a conventional Arab attack, Israel will be powerless to use its nuclear arsenal. Of course, Israel isn't exactly helpless, thanks to plenty of Euro debt extended to help them arm against aggression. *Jane's Intelligence Review* gives a status report on the Israeli military that should have Arab leaders worried. It rates Israel as the world's third–strongest military power. The Israeli Air Force is seven to eight times more powerful than all the air forces of the Arab world combined.

The Arabs are doing their best to catch up. They spent an average of 25% of their total national expenditure in 1996 on weapons and security hardware—all on credit, of course, and brought to you by the peace–loving international banking community as part of its contribution to the balance of power. Total Arab weapons purchases exceeded $156.6 billion.

Is this more conspiracy nonsense? Draw your own conclusions. An alliance of Syrian, Egyptian, Iraqi and Iranian forces is openly receiving military tactical support from Russia, a country barely able to pay its own army. Iran and Syria are stockpiling chemical weapons in preparation for a conflict with Israel. Israel has relied on its nuclear arsenal as a deterrent to an Arab invasion. The Arab stockpile of chemical weapons, a missile system capable of delivering those warheads, and Arab willingness to use such weapons, changes the equation. Israel's daily newspaper *Ha'aretz* said that nearly 9,000 Russian scientists and technicians are currently involved in various Iranian military projects. Israel's Channel 2 Television reported in August 1997 that Russian–Israeli relations had reached a crisis point over the missile project. But there is no way to hit the US with these weapons, and the US is Israel's principle protector. The detonation of a few nuclear suitcases would dampen American enthusiasm for interference in the next Middle East war. The fact that there are as many as 84 of these weapons, all of which could already be in place, dampens enthusiasm even more.

A EUROPEAN–RUSSIAN AXIS?

French President Jacques Chirac made an official three–day visit to Russia during the last week in September 1997. He was warmly greeted by the Russian leader, who expressed great interest in a Russian/French grand alliance. President Chirac told the Russians;

> "Like you, we want a special partnership between Russia and France. Russia and Europe, and a leading place for a strong and peaceful Russia in tomorrow's multi–polar world."[20]

That may not sound like much except diplomatic double-speak, but, under analysis, we hear a number of important code words. They spell bad news for US/Russian/European relations. To begin with, a "partnership" means more than friendly relations. A partnership is a relationship in which both sides work together toward their mutual self–interests. France is a heavy hitter in the European Union, and so Chirac's comments about including the EU in this partner-

---

[20] *International Intelligence Digest,* Intelligence International Ltd. The Stoneyhill Center. Brimpsfield, Gloucester LF48LF UK.

ship carry considerable weight. Another interesting code word is "multi–polar." That's a diplomatic buzzword used by states like Europe, Iran, Red China and Korea who want to see a world with a diminished American influence. Anti–Americanism is nothing new for France. The French have always preferred to call the shots, and they are not pleased with the status quo. They resent America's influence and believe the world would be better off if they had more to say in how it is run. That is one reason the French are so unflinchingly pro–Arab in the Arab–Israeli dispute. France is now committed to its goal of diminishing US influence—so committed, in fact, that it is willing to enter into an alliance with Russia, if that will accomplish its goal.

RUSSIA'S ANGLE

Since the collapse of the Cold War, Russia's economic situation has steadily deteriorated, to the degree that they are likely to ally themselves with anyone or any group in order to climb back up the ladder toward superpower status. The Russian psyche is deeply rooted in the concept of an all–powerful Mother Russia, always ready to rise from the ashes. Russia's Economic Analysis Institute issued its 1997 report, and the numbers were dismal. The 1997 Gross Domestic Product at $585 billion puts Great Mother Russia at well below superpower status. Russia ranks at roughly 14th in world economic output, far below European states like Germany at $1.478 trillion, or France at $1.201 trillion. Even tiny Italy, whose government life expectancy is routinely measured in weeks or months, enjoys a GDP of $1.123 trillion. That is a serious blow to Russian pride, and the Russian people are patriots in the extreme. The United States, once viewed worldwide as Russia's only credible challenge to global superpower status, output some $7.4 trillion in 1997, a figure that is a staggering 12 times the Russian effort. Russia finds itself on an economic par with Spain, whose GDP comes in at about $512 billion. The problem is, Russia doesn't see itself as Spain. The Russian people see themselves in the same way a 40 year old man might look in a mirror. The 40–year–old man might know he is 40, but the image he sees is not too different from what he saw when he was 21, young, virile, with a full head of hair and a washboard stomach. We see ourselves in the most favorable of lights, regardless of reality, and without noticing the ravages of time. Thus it is with nations, and Russia is no exception.

Across Russia, wages remain unpaid for months on end. The army is so demoralized and ill–equipped that one Russian official remarked, "The army is capable of mounting an honor guard around the Kremlin, but little more."

Following French President Jacques Chirac's overtures for a partnership with the Kremlin, the Russian self–image jumped considerably. President Boris Yeltsin took the offensive against what he sees as American arrogance. He even urged the exclusion of American representatives to the Council of Europe meeting in Strasbourg later that year. Yeltsin told reporters "We do not need an uncle from elsewhere. We ourselves can unite and live normally." Russians often use the expression "Uncle Sam" when referring to the United States.

Yeltsin's reaction was just what the European leaders wanted to hear. The gradual erosion of American dominance over financial and political concerns around the world fits with the geopolitical realities that have been engineered as part of the overall attempt to close the circle and return global hegemony to Europe, where it has always been.

CHAPTER SIX

THE NEW MONEY

"When you're in a community,

you have to try to reach a consensus

rather than imposing your point of view"

FRENCH FINANCE MINISTER JEAN ARTHUIS

OCTOBER 1997

SETTING THE STAGE

Europe's future economic plans rest on several "pillars." First among them is the concept of "interdependence." "Interdependence" simply means that each nation is regionalized, with no single nation being fully self sufficient. Different regions of the world are "centers" for raw materials; other regions are "centers" for manufacturing, or distribution, or as service sector economies. As a result, each region is "interdependent" on other regions to get their goods or services to market. The profits then travel through various currency exchanges, or banking centers, with a point or two shaved off at each way station. Interdependence ensures no single country or region is in a position to dictate terms too loudly, or become totally independent of the banking system that feeds it. A deregulation deal signed between 191 countries and the World Trade Organization pledged each member country to divest itself of state–held monopolies. Since the agreement was signed, deregulation barriers have begun to fall. The effect of deregulation is most clearly seen by Americans who now have a choice which phone company they use, for example. Politicians sold the deal to their constituents by promising them lower phone bills. But the money governments used to collect from their monopolies has to come from somewhere. Lower phone bills will ultimately be followed by notices of tax increases. But at the top of the food chain, deregulation is exposed as just another global confidence scheme. MCI—the long–distance company—was a product of deregulation. British Telecommunications bought MCI in 1997, over the objections of the US Justice Department. British Telecom broke up its internal monopoly in favor of a global monopoly. The merger created a super phone company with revenues of $42 billion spread across 72 countries. Deregulation at the local level is just a smokescreen to hide the largest global takeover of telecommunications in history. The promise of lower telephone bills through deregulation is little more than a bribe. What we are actually seeing is the result of long range planning. Here's how it works. The ultimate goal is the control of the global economy. The plan was set in motion with the GATT Treaty signed in 1948 in Europe. GATT became the World Trade Organization in 1995. The WTO was the sponsor of the global deregulation scheme. The actual plan can be summed up by the bumper sticker phrase so many of us proudly stick on our cars. The slogan "think globally, act locally" is more than just a catchy phrase. It's the bottom line. Telecommunications is the key to controlling the global economy. The global economy moves around the world across the telephone lines. Whoever controls global telecommunications therefore controls the global economy. That's an awful lot of power to put into the hands of any one company. The fact that the global takeover is sponsored by a former European state–owned monopoly is just a coincidence—a carefully planned coincidence that took 50 years to accomplish.

WILL THAT BE DEBIT OR CHARGE?

The second "pillar" holding up Europe's global economic future is the single currency unit. There are just too many national currencies to afford total control to a global central banking scheme—at least for the time being. A single currency system is necessary—and then only as a stop–gap measure. We'll look at efforts to bring that into reality a little later, but, first things first.

Ultimately, the only system that will give total control of the economy to the bankers—who genuinely believe that is the only option to ensure global prosperity—is one that eliminates cash altogether. A cashless society will be a hard sell in many parts of the world, but there is a viable plan. Once again we see the specter of managed crisis looming on the horizon. Not too long ago, the idea of a cashless society seemed as unreal as the likelihood that there would ever actually be a global economy. It has only been since the Crash of 1987 that the "global economy" concept has even been openly discussed, despite the obvious signs it had already been in existence for some time. Americans tended to believe we lived and worked and earned and saved American dollars in an American system. Cash was the coin of the realm, untraceable, anonymous and safe. But over the last ten years, new forms of commerce have been steadily making inroads toward universal public acceptance. Using their economic control of the media, the global economic planners have introduced the public to the miracles of electronic commerce. Debit cards have largely replaced checks. TV commercials depict people who write checks as obstacles to the speedy conduction of transactions. One commercial in particular contrasts two women who each have to catch a train. One stops at a store and has to write a check. While the announcer's voice drones in the background about the time and inconvenience, the viewer is given flashes of the people waiting impatiently behind her. She writes the check, (taking far too long), fumbles for identification (apparently, this woman is the most disorganized person on Planet Earth), waits until the equally inefficient clerk checks her ID (the line behind her grows longer and increasingly impatient) until, finally, the harried clerk clears the transaction and the woman is on her way. The other woman (better dressed, more efficient, and obviously a superior human being) merely pulls out an XYZ bank debit card, slides it through an electronic reader and is on her way. The clerk is really not even necessary, except to serve as an official greeter and to thank her for her intelligence, wit, and charm, and to admire her for the wisdom she displays by using the debit card instead of the check. The line behind her stops just short of giving her a round of applause and voting her "Woman of the Year" on the spot. The spot ends with the question, "Which one of these women caught the train?" The subliminal message is obvious. Anyone who uses a debit card is superior, efficient and successful. People who prefer the traditional method of writing checks are losers. Which would you rather be?

You may be wondering the obvious. Isn't there a third option? Why didn't she just whip out a $20 bill and pay for her purchases even more quickly? Or get up a few minutes earlier, so she could buy whatever she needed and still catch the train on time? But if you watch the commercial, carefully crafted by professional advertising psychologists, you never get that far. Instead, you begin to feel the same way about people in line who waste your time writing checks when they could be using debit cards instead. The advertising blitz goes on. Another TV spot shows comedian Jerry Seinfeld buying gasoline at a self–serve station. He "over-pumps" (whatever that means), and the viewer is terrified, along with Seinfeld, that he might actually have to wait for his change. Instead, Seinfeld slides his debit card into the pump's electronic reader, and he is on his way. The camera doesn't follow him to his next destination, presumably to conceal the fact that he won't have a quarter for the parking meter (some things still haven't entered the digital revolution).

ENTER THE INTERNET SYSTEM

The global economy is turning its attention to the growing electronic marketplace, and the big banks are making sure they are ready. Visa and MasterCard have developed a joint project called the "Secure Electronic Transactions Protocol" for the Internet. The new Internet banking system is called SetCo. Consumers worry about hackers intercepting their credit cards when they make purchases over the Internet. The protocol is designed to make credit card purchases over the Internet safe. The Secure Electronic Transactions, or SET, has already been endorsed by American Express, Diners Club, Novus, and Air Travel Card.

SetCo also has plans to develop future versions of SET for use with smart cards and additional debit card options. Ten years ago, a cashless society seemed impossible, especially among freedom loving Americans concerned for their financial privacy. Today consumers are demanding banks drop ATM fees so they can increase their use of Electronic Fund Transfer technology. The banks, who save billions using ATM's that never sleep, and work 24 hours a day for the cost of electricity, created an artificial "surcharge" for no apparent reason other than to inflame public opinion against the industry and to increase demand for access to ATM machines. EFT technology means no tellers, no bank buildings, no cash to count, print, handle or store, no checks, no paperwork, just electronic entries in a computer. It also provides a method to track all purchases, control access to capital, and would all but eliminate the underground economy.

HOW DID THAT HAPPEN?

In order to complete the plan to eliminate cash, public

perception has to be focused on an enemy, and the enemy is good old anonymous cash. To accomplish this, the "dangers" of anonymity must make daily headlines. For example, America is trillions of dollars in debt, as we already know. Politicians say the reason is because of the untaxed dollars that circulate through the underground economy. Treasury officials say eliminating cash would bring in hundreds of billions in tax dollars currently circulating untracked in the underground "cash only" economy. The application of laws like Cash Transaction Reports and the development of agencies like FINCEN are also geared to force a public outcry for the elimination of cash. We have already found that the money laundering industry is the third largest on earth. More money is spent for drugs each year than food. Drug lords deal in suitcases full of $100 bills, and money laundering can be a very efficient operation. But, without cash, how will a drug dealer turn a profit? No junkie is going to be willing to pay for his next high using an electronic transfer card that can track his purchases. No drug dealer is going to set up a credit card or debit card station. The drug trade could conceivably be eliminated overnight by the simple expediency of eliminating cash. At least, in theory, if not in practice. Criminals are resourceful enough to figure out a way to get around the problems presented. Our look at the BCCI scandal proves there are sufficiently greedy men in the right political and financial circles to ensure they do. But in the meantime, it makes a convincing argument for public consumption. Over time, the public will demand that governments and banks figure out a way to eradicate cash from the equation. A powerful argument can be made that eliminating cash would eliminate drugs, money laundering schemes, political corruption, and would eventually result in a utopian society. Politicians would have to keep their hands clean. An electronic trail is impossible to conceal, considering electronic money can't exist without it.

What it really means is that banks and the banking system will no longer have to share their profits with the competition. They'd have it all, nice and legal, easy and cheap, and they'd be doing a public service.

THE NEXT GLOBAL POWER ISN'T POLITICAL

Thirdly, Europe's political future must be dictated by the central banking system. The World Economic Forum met in Davos, Switzerland, in 1997 to map the global economic plan for the new millennium. It was apparent early on that the major players at Davos were not American politicians; they weren't even European politicians. In fact, they weren't politicians at all. I suppose that is to be expected; it is, after all, a World Economic Forum. The politicians that were there were tokens, more to pick up their marching orders than to dictate the battle plans. When Newt Gingrich took his turn at the speaker's podium, there were plenty of empty seats. But it was standing room only when finance ministers and central bank governors from Europe took their turns.

THE NEW "GLOBAL POWER"

The world is on the brink of seeing the promised European Monetary Union come to pass—and it will come to pass, whether politicians like it or not. This is truly the dawn of a new world order, a time when politics will be driven by the economy, and economic policy will set the political agendas.

It sounds a little "over the top" when you put it into words, but that doesn't change reality. European Commission President Jacques Santer told the gathering he looks forward to the day when Europe becomes a "global power." The route he plans to take to global power is paved with European Monetary Units, not dollars, yen or Deutsche marks. Monetary union is everything to Europe's plans, and it can't work unless all members meet the terms set forth by the citizens of Europe in the Maastricht referendums. So, sometimes it's necessary to get creative. Former French President and Euro–enthusiast Valery Giscard d'Estaing suggests something called "conditional acceptance" to Italy and Spain, despite the fact both countries are unable to comply with EU rules for national solvency. As he told the *Paris International Herald Tribune* (Feb. 13, 1997), "It is highly important that Italy and Spain be members of the first wave of countries launching the euro." He said that "naturally Italy and Spain can only be admitted if they meet the criteria contained in the Maastricht treaty," but he has a solution. You see, the Maastricht treaty calls for each participating nation to be financially solvent by the time of monetary integration. Without that condition, the voters of the wealthier countries would never have approved the 1992 Maastricht referendum. That would have ended plans for an integrated Europe by 2000. The voters approved the union under those terms. So d'Estaing proposes a little currency manipulation—just a little. And who knows, maybe he'll pick up a few bucks along the way.

WHO RUNS THE NEW EUROPE?

Now things are up to the European Commission. The European Commission serves as the executive branch of the EU. Its members are not directly elected by anyone, but are appointed by agreement among member governments. The Commission's prime directive is economic, so its membership is drawn from the cream of European banking. In other words, the European Union's executive branch is composed entirely of unelected bankers. Political policies are made there and then handed down to the politicians for implementation. The only European government body directly elected by its citizens is the 567–member European Parliament, a legislative body whose composition, by design, makes meaningful legislation all but impossible. In short, Europe represents the future of government—a government of the banking establishment, by the banking establishment, and for the banking establishment. To the betterment of the people, of course.

$$$ MAKES THE WORLD GO 'ROUND

The proof that economic alliances take precedence over political alliances becomes more apparent all the time. For four decades, a country not on good terms with America would find itself shut out of most of the world's capitals. No longer. Despite the decades–long American embargo, you can still buy a good Cuban cigar anywhere in Canada. Havana is the vacation spot of choice from Toronto to Vancouver. Europe has already hauled the United States before the World Trade Organization (a sort of global Supreme Court for bankers) to complain about US policy toward Cuba. The US says Cuba is a security matter, not an economic one, so it is outside the WTO's jurisdiction. Au contraire, says Europe. In the words of EU Trade Minister Leon Brittan, "For such a system to work, it must not be possible for one country to evade its operation by proclaiming its national security is involved."

In the New World Economic Order, national security takes second place, behind trade. Even American national security. Now, the idea of conquering Cuban troops marching up Pennsylvania Avenue is a little bizarre, but that's why this is the test case. Because the national security issue sounds so weak!

POLITICS VS. ECONOMICS

Meanwhile, Europe has already signed unilateral trade agreements with Yasser Arafat and a nonexistent Palestinian State. The French are selling weapons systems to Iran, the Germans are selling restricted chemicals to Iraq, and Iran and Iraq have teamed up and are selling embargoed Iraqi oil to everyone. Vice Adm. Thomas B. Fargo, commander of the US 5th Fleet, said Iraq is selling at bargain prices, and Iran is taking a cut. When there is enough money on the table, anything is possible, politics or no.

Turkey enjoys warm relations with the US. It has also entered into joint defense initiatives with Israel. That means Turkey does not have the warmest of relations with the Arab Middle East where all the oil is. Europe has been busy courting Arab favor. It started with the pro–Western government of Turkey back in 1960. Turkey was guaranteed full membership in the EU—in writing. But Europe is getting along with the Arabs just fine, thanks to the US support of Israel in the peace talks. Now friendship with Turkey is a liability to improved relations among the Arabs. When Turkey applied for full membership in 1997, the EU rejected Turkey's application—no reason given. US endorsements are not what they used to be.

The British are still uncomfortable with the idea of surrendering their currency to Europe. On January 29, 1997, Tokyo informed Britain that if it failed to sign on by the 1999 deadline, it would be unlikely to invest further in the UK. Soon after, Britain announced it was dropping its objections to monetary union.

A GOOD KING OR A BAD KING?

It really boils down to one simple question, "So what?" The bankers seem to be doing a pretty good job. Since they started openly running things, Europe has prospered. Germany hasn't tried to expand its borders or begin a new world war. American national security isn't really threatened by Canadians buying Cuban cigars. And if the European bankers on the European Commission are skimming a little off the top, who cares, so long as there is enough for everybody. So maybe it's a good thing.

At least, so it seems. Remember, Adolf Hitler turned the German economy around in less than a decade. He built the autobahn, introduced the Volkswagen, and made the trains run on time.

Europe has surrendered overall control to the economists. In so doing, they have surrendered representative government in fact in favor of representative government in form only. The new European system resembles nothing so much as a kingdom, with the king holding his court on the 13th floor of the European Commission headquarters in Brussels. Will he be a good king or a bad king?

Because that is what will determine whether there will be feast or famine across Europe—and across America. As we pass the threshold into the next millennium, you'll hear much about the transformation of China, or a free trade zone in Singapore or Hong Kong—and, all of that is very important. But, if you want to know in what direction our future is truly headed, watch Europe.

CHAPTER SEVEN

THE RING OF FIRE

"My favorite advice is

'Don't worry, be happy.'

Is this going to last forever?

Of course not."

DAVIS WYSS, SENIOR FINANCIAL ECONOMIST
AT & STANDARD & POOR'S DRI
APRIL 21, 1998

The Pacific Rim countries (PACRIM) are often referred to as the "ring of fire" due to the circle of active volcanoes that surround them. Generally speaking, the "ring of fire" includes the Andes of South America, the volcanoes of Central America, the Cascades and Aleutians of North America, the volcanoes of the Kamchatka Peninsula and Kuriles in Eastern Russia, Japan, the Izu and Mariana islands, the Philippines, Indonesia, Papua New Guinea, Tonga, Kermadek, and New Zealand. Financially, these countries are even hotter than their reputation.

The financial markets of Southeast Asia are awash with anxiety. It seems that many investors fear the Asian banking system is out of control, and nobody has enough clout to do anything about it. The International Monetary Fund has been active in the region. At a meeting of the Association of Southeast Asian Nations, the IMF laid down some guidelines in exchange for a promise of a bailout package from the global bank.

The ministers of the ASEAN nations reacted angrily, calling it a form of economic dictatorship. But something has to be done. In Indonesia, rumors of an impending bank failure drove the local currency down some 9% against the dollar in a single day in late October 1997. In Malaysia, the country's largest savings institution nearly succumbed to a two–day run on the bank amid rumors its founder had died. In Thailand, the government has already closed 58 of its 91 finance companies. Moody's Investor's group is predicting as many as a third of Thailand's leading banks will fail by the end of 1998.

Part of the problem stems from the haphazard way in which bankers evaluate suitable candidates for loans.

DICTATORS R US

For example, former Indonesian President–for–life Suharto is demanding a $690 million loan for a national car project. Indonesia feels it needs to be able to manufacture its own Indonesian automobile. Suharto's plan is to put his youngest son, Tommy, in partnership with South Korea's debt–ridden Kia Motors. Odds are good Suharto will get the loan. On the other hand, its not likely Indonesia will ever get a national car. Or that the financing bank will ever see its money again.

Indonesia's central bank is typical of many banking institutions in Southeast Asia. The Summa Bank remains in operation, despite the fact that it failed in 1992 and stuck the central bank of Indonesia with $180 million in bad paper. The same applies to the Bank Pacific, also partly owned by the central bank. Bank Pacific's president, the daughter of a Suharto ally, had her bank guarantee loans taken by a finance company she also controlled. Surprise, surprise, those loans are in arrears, and there is nobody to collect from. Banks in China, Japan and South Korea are currently sitting on billions in bad loans. For a time, rapid economic growth and exceptionally high domestic savings rates hid the flaws in the runaway Southeast Asian market. It worked like a pyramid scheme. The ASEAN banks pegged their exchange rate favorably against the dollar to keep the foreign investment flowing. There was plenty of money, at first, to pay investors, provided they brought in new investors. But finding new investors is becoming increasingly difficult. Rejecting the demands of the IMF and World Bank to put their financial house in order further reduced ASEAN's attractiveness to foreign money. Now the investors are looking for a new place to put their money. Little by little, it's flowing into Europe. Which is really no surprise, as we'll see.

THE HONG KONG HANDOVER

On July 1, 1997, with much pomp and circumstance, the People's Republic of China formally took control of Hong Kong. The handover is the realization of an agreement signed between Britain and China back in 1984. Here is a little background. Britain took control of Hong Kong as part of the spoils of war following the 19th century Great Opium War. That war was fought because British merchants wanted to import opium into China. The British won the right to control the opium trade and Hong Kong in 1840. A Second Opium War in 1860 ended when the British occupied Beijing and the summer palace. That part of history isn't taught much in Western schools, but every Chinese school-boy knows it inside out.

THE BIG PICTURE

China's takeover of Hong Kong opened a wound that has been festering for 150 years. But in order to understand the big picture, we have to look at the big picture—warts and all. The fact that Hong Kong was the prize in a war between drug dealers in the 1840s makes great propaganda. Many Chinese feel the handover is justice long overdue. And it's a convincing argument. Except for one detail. This isn't 1840, and the issue isn't drugs anymore. It's all about money. Hong Kong controls the seventh largest economy in the world. Many Western observers think that is reason enough to believe Hong Kong will change China and not the other way around. That is optimism carried to the level of absurdity. The foundation of Hong Kong's business success is Chinese investment. Mainland China is home to half the world's population. On July 1, 1997, it looked like they were all marching into Hong Kong at once.

THE BIGGEST MARKET IN THE WORLD

Even if you leave out all the poor people in China—and there are a lot—the people's republic represents a tremendous market. That's one reason American business leaders are romancing Chinese President Jiang Zemin. China's middle–class alone—people with the wherewithal to buy Coca–Colas and Jeep Cherokees—is roughly equal to the populations of Italy, France and the United Kingdom combined, or of the buying public in the United States. The difference is that we already have most of the stuff we want to sell. Chinese middle–classers are eager to fill empty shelves. It is a virgin market, yearning to be tapped. Imagine a country where a billion people wake up each morning craving what you sell. That is what the People's Republic of Red China represents. **"There are a lot of Chinese who are doing very well, and can afford to build expensive houses, take expensive vacations and buy Gucci handbags,"** says Eliot Clauss, president of the US–China Chamber of Commerce after a visit to Red China. **"The coastal provinces and the major cities account for a market of 200 million, a market the size of the United States. A real consumer market is developing."** One company, Boeing, signed a deal in 1997 to sell $3 billion worth of airplanes to China. Still, China offers businesses all sorts of impediments to making money there. China has barriers to American exports—duties, quotas, import licenses, and insists that US companies deal through

Chinese state enterprises. Partly as a result, China sells $6 worth of products or services in the United States for every $1 worth of American products or services sold in China. Moreover, American companies find that doing business with China has worrisome long–term consequences. The Chinese do not want to buy Chevys made in Detroit. They want Chevys made in China—in Chinese factories, by Chinese labor with most of the profit staying in China. That sort of thing can cause troubles for US firms, as well as for the US government. Money talks, as they say. **"Investment in China has come at a real price,"** says Greg Mastel, China expert at the Economic Strategy Institute. **"China has demanded the transfer of production technology. Against their will, companies are being forced to help build up their Chinese competitors."** All this economic muscle also gives China the ability to demand supercomputers, nuclear technology and other sensitive or strategic information and hardware, despite the clear and present danger it presents to US interests abroad, particularly among the rogue nations of the Middle East.

The United States suspects China sells the stuff of nuclear weaponry to countries such as Iran, Washington has prevented the US nuclear power industry—starved for customers now that nuclear power has gone out of fashion in this country—from selling to China, a potential $60 billion market. Money has no allegiances.

MONEY IS A WEAPON

Britain's conquest of Hong Kong is an ugly piece of history. China continues to compete in the marketplace with goods made by slave labor in prisons. It continues to pirate

Western technology, reselling it on the open market. That is
not something the masters of the global economy are likely
to overlook. China's human rights record is among the
worst in the world. That's an issue that will come back to
haunt them in the years ahead. A little money in the right
place can change more minds than the barrel of a gun.
Money is a weapon. And Hong Kong is the economic
equivalent to a nuclear warhead. When China inherited
Hong Kong, it also inherited Hong Kong's wealth. Hong
Kong had been the third largest holder of US debt in the
world. Now Red China occupies that position. The British
government handed over Hong Kong for a reason, and we
can be certain that the Bank of England had considerable
sway over that decision. The Bank of England is America's
number–one creditor. Public opinion may be that the UK's
economy is faltering, but don't believe everything you read
in the papers. The same applies to China. The adage "he
who has the gold makes the rules" is still true. If China suddenly announced plans to divest itself of American paper,
the US stock market would come tumbling down like a
house of cards. Britain remains poised to pick up the pieces.
What Nathan Rothschild accomplished in 1815 after the
Battle of Waterloo was no fluke of history. The United
States found itself an economic hostage overnight to an
enemy it can't appease forever. A little push here, a nudge
there, and Europe could easily find itself holding even more
American paper. To ensure things go as planned, Yukon
Huang, a former governor of the International Monetary
Fund, is now head of China's central bank. With one of their
own in control of the checkbook, all that separates America
from bankruptcy is its willingness to look the other way.
When the time is right, even that won't help.

WEALTH EQUALS POWER

We can see how China's new–found wealth works as a weapon by looking in our own back yard. During the "Chinagate Scandal," CIA agent John Dickerson testified before Congress regarding DNC fundraiser John Huang. The agent told Congress he interviewed Huang 37 times during the course of Huang's fund–raising activities. His comments came following a suit filed by the group Judicial Watch. The suit alleges the sale of seats on Commerce Department trade missions to political donors. Huang got a top–secret clearance five months before joining the Commerce Deptartment. At the time, he was an official of a Lippo Bank in LA. Judicial Watch claims Huang's ties to the Indonesian Lippo Group were a conflict of interests. The head of the Lippo Group, James Riady, is a long time friend of President Clinton. Huang also has extensive business interests in China. Representative John Solomon of New York charged that "electronic intercepts show Mr. Huang committed economic espionage and breached our national security" by passing classified data to Lippo. Records show that on two occasions, Mr. Huang received documents classified as "secret" followed by three telephone calls to the Lippo Bank in Los Angeles. On one of those occasions, he also scheduled a meeting with Chinese officials. With Huang's help, Chinese arms dealers had cozy visits with the President while the CIA was occupied trying to stem the flow of AK47's into the USA. The CIA agent told Congress Huang kept an exceptionally neat desk and did not seem as busy as other Commerce officials. "There was an air of inactivity about his office," he said. After Huang left the Commerce Department, he became a top fund–raiser at the

Democratic Party. He joined the DNC following a meeting at the White House with the president and James Riady. Money can't buy love, it seems, but everything else is up for grabs.

THE UK'S ON FIRST. CHINA'S ON THIRD. WHO'S ON SECOND?

US debt is financed through the sale of Treasury bills and other promissory notes. Anybody who owns US savings bonds, for example, owns a portion of the debt. Taken individually, each note isn't of much consequence. But recently, a comment by Japanese Prime Minister Hashimoto that suggested Japan may sell off its US securities sent the stock market into temporary free fall. That's because, collectively, Japan holds a tremendous number of US securities. Japan is the second–largest holder of US securities in the world. And that gives Japan economic leverage and power over the US economy.

ASLEEP AT THE SWITCH

The United States, through the Federal Reserve, sold that power to the Japanese government in much the same way and for the same reasons that we might sell a car to our neighbor. Once the deal is done and the title is transferred, ownership and control of the car now belongs to that neighbor. The US freely sold that power to Japan, knowing that Japan's economic fortunes are intermingled with our own. Anything Japan does to hurt the US economy hurts Japan. A kind of economic Mutually Assured Destruction scenario. But the Japanese economy is in trouble. While we may be on friendly terms with Japan, there's a saying in economic circles that goes something like, "A friend in need is a pain in the neck."

A PAPER TIGER

Until the early 1990s, Japan was being regarded as an Eastern peril. Many felt the Japanese were buying America wholesale. But when the Japanese economy took a downturn, fewer Japanese investors were showing up in American real estate offices. Most Americans took it as a sign that, somehow, we had regained control of our economy. Once again, the American good ship Enterprise was riding high on a wave of investor confidence.

Until the Japanese PM made the following statement. **"We hope,"** he said, **"the US will engage in efforts to maintain foreign exchange stability so we don't have to succumb to the temptation to sell off US Treasury bills."** The next day, the Dow plunged 192 points, the second biggest daily loss in US history.

Hashimoto said later his remarks were misinterpreted, but that's not the point. The point is, for a second, just for a second, we got a peek at our real economic picture. We are balancing our books by counting T–bills as money instead of what they really are. IOU's. Japan holds enough of them to trigger a minor panic with a misplaced word. It proves the unthinkable—but unvarnished—truth. The economy is a paper tiger, and countries like Japan, or Europe, are holding a box of matches. If they ever strike one, the economic miracle of the '90s will be exposed for what it really is. Smoke and mirrors. When the smoke clears, the mirror will reflect the real value of our paper millions. Europe, through the Bank of England, controls a significant majority of American debt. There is little doubt that some selective deal–making that brought Hong Kong back into the Chinese fold gave the international financial community some leverage over China's share of Washington's bounced checks. A Japanese bailout would constitute the Grand Slam of international finance. The Ring of Fire could easily close—around Uncle Sam's neck.

JAPAN'S LOOSE CANNON

Japan's economic reality hovers above our heads like a Sword of Damocles. Japanese investment in US real estate played a large part in America's recovery from the recession of the '70s and '80s. Japanese cash provided money for investment and economic growth at a time when American capital was totally occupied in maintaining our status quo. Japanese investment in America wasn't made for nothing. American industry was still the best place to demonstrate faith in the US's phoenix–like ability to rise from the ashes, better and stronger than before. Japanese investors knew that their money was in good hands until they needed it. The problem is, Japan needs a large portion of it now, and we're not done using it yet. The 1997 Asian monetary crisis demonstrated to investors just how vulnerable we became to the vagaries of fortune on the other side of the world. The backlash against Japanese investment reached a fever pitch during the late 1980s, when American resentment of the fact we willingly sold our birthright to foreign investment began to sink in. What never really took hold was the fact that someday we'd have to redeem the paper that Japan under-wrote so willingly. Well, the future, as they say, is *now*. As the Japanese market struggles back from its daily trip to the brink, Wall Street holds its breath. At the end of each business day, the sigh of relief in New York can be heard all the way to San Francisco. As Jon Olesky, head of Morgan Stanley Dean Witter told the *Wall Street Journal*, **"This is the downside of being a global market."**[21]

If ever there was a comment that could truly lay claim to the title "understatement of the century," that certainly would be a top contender! Japan's holdings in the United States are vast. The US economy is battered by a huge trade imbalance with Japan. Japan has maintained its position as the region's powerhouse, backed by almost $230 billion in foreign exchange reserves. That's four times the amount held by the United States—and a lofty current account surplus. In other words, we are bailing out an economy that has four times as much cash as we do. Where are we getting the money from? Why, we're borrowing it! The question is, why? And the answer is frightening. We already owe it to the Japanese in the form of securities. Now we need to borrow it from somewhere else to keep our loans from being called in. In the worst case, mounting troubles in Japan could prompt cash–strapped banks to sell their US Treasury bond holdings. That would raise bond yields up, bringing the stock market down. According to Treasury data, Japan holds an estimated $320 billion in US government securities. That amounts to 9.5% of all privately held debt. Such is the state of interdependence between the two nations, that, although on the other side of the world, we are more like a married couple than competitors in the global marketplace. In the same sense that a spouse buying a new car might end the other spouse's dream of a vacation, when the Japanese market takes a dip, it comes directly from the pockets of American investors—and, ultimately, directly out of the savings of the American people.

---

[21] *Wall Street Journal,* October 24, 1997.

Because of the enormity of Japanese investment in US hold-ings, the reduction of the value of the yen is directly related to the value of the dollar. When the yen drops, Japanese goods become cheaper. American goods become more expensive to buy. US manufacturers suffer in the domestic market.

"American business has responded much more than in the early 1980s, the last time the dollar moved up sharply. This time it cut costs, shaved prices and profit margins, developed products, sold harder. The unex-pected export vigor has added significantly to the nation's sales, here and abroad, and has bolstered the economy, helping to prolong the expansion into its sev-enth year. American manufacturers have managed to export against the odds," said Wynne Godley, an econo-mist at the Jerome Levy Institute, a research group. At the same time, however, the robust dollar makes it easier and less costly for America's trading partners to export more to this country, and they are doing just that. Despite the rapid growth in American exports, foreign companies are selling more in the United States than American business sells abroad. The turmoil in Southeast Asia, with its currencies falling in value, will only increase these sales to America.[22]

The resulting trade imbalance means the only ones who make any money are the money traders who get paid no matter which side of the ocean they make their deals on.

COUNTDOWN TO MELTDOWN

When the Asian stock markets rejected the offers of the IMF and World Bank to step in and take control of their

---

[22] *New York Times,* October 31, 1997.

economies, a line was drawn in the sand, so to speak. The impudence of rejecting the generous offer made by the controllers of the money elite was just too unkind a cut to bear without an appropriate response. But the response had to fit the provocation. And, if handled properly, there was some money to be made along the way. The global economic planners employed a tried–and–true method of bringing Asia back into line, using the old "management by crisis" system that has worked so well in the past. The "little dragon" nations of the ASEAN free trade zone fought back, but it was like trying to beat back a hurricane with a stick. Here is a brief chronological countdown to the Far Eastern Meltdown of 1997.

- May 14: Thailand's currency, the baht, is hit by a wave of selling by speculators who move in response to economic woes and political instability. Thailand and Singapore intervene to defend the baht, but Thailand refuses to devalue it. The Philippines is affected as well; the central bank raises the overnight lending interest rate 1.75 percentage points, to 13%, and unloads dollars.

- June 19: Thai Finance Minister Amnuay Viravan, an opponent of devaluation, resigns, and Thailand's stock market falls 4%. The resignation spurs the Philippines to raise the overnight lending rate to 15%.

- June 27: Thailand's central bank suspends operations of 16 cash–strapped finance companies and orders them to submit merger or consolidation plans.

- June 30: Thai Prime Minister Chavalit Yonchaiyudh assures the nation the baht will not be devalued.

- July 2: Thailand lets the baht float freely against other currencies, in effect devaluing it by 15 to 20% to a record low of 28.80 to the dollar. The Philippine central bank intervenes to defend the peso.

- July 3: The Philippine central bank raises the overnight rate to 24%.

- July 8: Malaysia's central bank intervenes to defend the ringgit. The currency hits a high of 2.5100/10 after a low of 2.5240/50.

- July 11: The Philippine central bank allows the peso to move in a wider range against the dollar. The Indonesian rupiah starts to be affected, and Indonesia loosens controls on the currency's trading range.

- July 14: The IMF offers the Philippines almost $1.1 billion in emergency loans.

- July 24: A currency meltdown sweeps Southeast Asia. The Malaysian ringgit hits 38–month low of 2.6530 to the dollar and Malaysian Prime Minister Mahathir Mohamad launches a bitter attack on "rogue speculators." The Hong Kong dollar remains steady, but the territory later reveals that $1 billion was spent on intervention during a period of two hours on an unspecified day in July.

- July 26: Mahathir blames American trader George Soros for the ringgit's fall. Soros later calls Mahatir a "menace to his own country."

- Aug. 5: Thailand announces austerity measures and closes dozens of finance firms in an effort to secure the IMF loan package.

- Aug. 11: Thailand is pledged $16 billion in loans in a rescue package led by the IMF and Japan.

- Aug. 13: Indonesia's rupiah hits a historic low of 2,682 to the dollar before ending at 2,655. The central bank actively intervenes in its defense.

- Aug. 14: Indonesia loosens controls on the rupiah, and the currency plunges further to 2,755.

- Sept. 4: The Philippine peso falls to a record low of 32.43 to the dollar before the central bank intervenes. It ends at 32.38. Malaysia's Mahathir delays several multi–billion–dollar construction projects.

- Sept. 16: Indonesia postpones projects worth 39 trillion rupiah in an attempt to slash the budget shortfall.

- Sept. 20: Mahathir tells delegates to the IMF–World Bank annual conference in Hong Kong that currency trading is immoral and should be stopped.

- Oct. 1: Mahathir repeats his call for tighter regulation, or a total ban, on foreign exchange trading. The currency falls 4% in less than two hours.

- Oct. 6: The rupiah hits a low of 3,845.

- Oct. 8: Indonesia says it will ask the IMF for financial assistance.

- Oct. 14: Vietnam, bowing to months of pressure on its currency, the dong, doubles the permitted trading range to 10% either side of the daily official rate.

- Oct. 17: Malaysia presents a belt–tightening budget to try to stop the economy from sliding into recession.

- Oct. 20–23: Hong Kong's stock market loses nearly a quarter of its value in four days on fears over interest rates and pressures on the Hong Kong dollar.

The stage was set. The global planners planted their gardens well, and it was time to do a little weeding. It was also time to uproot a few of those blasphemous upstarts who dared to call currency trading "immoral." Didn't they know who they were talking to? The IMF bailouts that did come were just a little too late to help those in trouble, but they did arrive just in time to forestall a complete global collapse. Still, it was a foretaste of things to come. In terms of the global economy, nobody is neutral. Either you are part of the system, or you aren't. In other words, if you don't want to play ball by our rules, fine. But never forget whose ball it actually is.

THE GREAT BAILOUT OF 1997

When the Asian markets began to crumble, the world looked to Japan to take up the position of leadership. After years of promises to reform its economy and get off the ground, Japan continued to flirt with recession, as if it felt it was somehow protected against its fallout. Its international economic policy was so directionless that Tokyo lacked the clout to even point the way to a bailout of Thailand, the epi-center of Asia's currency crisis. At the time of this writing, its financial system is in such shambles that the survival of some big players is questionable. This really matters to the rest of the globe. With growth slowing in Asia and threatening to cool in America, the world needs Japan's $5 trillion economy to pick up any slack. But instead of addressing its woes head–on, Japan is dithering. Take the problem of hundreds of billions of dollars' worth of outstanding bad loans stretching back to the bubble economy of the 1980s. Japanese authorities hoped that banks would use time and low interest rates, instead of massive asset sales and restructuring, to heal balance sheets. Finally, the Japanese had no choice but to give in to the demands of the World Bank and IMF. As the fallout from the rest of Asia's markets began to reverberate across the Nikkei Exchange, Japan reluctantly dropped its objection to allowing its largest banking institutions to collapse under the weight of their own bad debts. Throughout the crisis, both the IMF and World Bank leaders demanded that the largest and most prolific lenders across Asia be liquidated. The surface argument in favor of "allowing" these banks to fail was to increase investor confidence in those banks which remained. Of course, it afforded the parallel of decreasing competition among the remaining banking establishments. Most of whom were at least partially owned by the same banks that control the IMF and World Bank. The methodology is easy enough to follow. In 1997, Thailand saw the value of its currency plummet 36%. Its stock market has lost 52% of its value. Malaysia's money was worth 28% less than it was at the beginning of the year. Its stock market dropped 56%. Malaysia's Prime Minister blamed the problem on foreign investment. It was Malaysian defiance of the World Bank and IMF demands that caused the dominoes to begin to topple. Indonesia's corrupt government made dozens of bad loans that eventually caused its currency to lose 35% of its value and devalued its stock market by 37%. Widespread corruption in the Philippines and huge banking losses from bad debts reduced its currency by 25% and crushed its stock values by a whopping 44%. South Korea's currency lost more than a quarter of its value. Its stocks were worth 37% less than they were at the beginning of the year. On the other hand, Japan, who is getting all the bad press, is really not as bad off as most people think. Although its currency was down, it only declined 10%. That's a lot, but not compared to most the rest of Asia. As this book is being written, the Nikkei index was only off 14%. But Japan is holding some $220 billion in bad paper, mostly in real estate loans. The Japanese banking industry has traditionally been propped up by the government. That is now a thing of the past. The International Monetary Fund developed a "quick–fix" plan to bailout troubled economies in late 1997. The new plan signalled a sharp shift in IMF bailouts, shortening their duration and raising the interest rate charged to borrowing governments to encourage a quick return to private capital markets. The IMF has been at the center of several multi–billion–dollar bailouts since the 1994–1995 Mexican peso crisis, which for the first time put the global financial policeman in the position of having to deal with a huge, sudden exodus of private capital from a vulnerable developing nation. In 1997 alone, the IMF helped assemble a $17 billion package for Thailand, an $18 billion bailout for Indonesia and a $57 billion rescue for South Korea. Through the mechanism of Supplemental Reserve Facility, recipient countries would have to pay interest rates between two and four percentage points above the usual subsidized IMF rate, which now stands at about 4.7%. Great deal for the lenders. Not so good for already battered developing nation's economies. But, business is business, and bankers are not known for their philanthropy. But in order to qualify, recipient nations must surrender control of their banking policies to the center, including "allowing" banks to fail at the whim of the IMF. A look into the ownership of those banks that do fail under IMF dictates have something in common. They don't belong to the global money trust.

Do you notice a pattern here?

WHO IS THE WORLD BANK?

The IMF and World Bank are both banking institutions heavily controlled by those same few banking giants that control the Federal Reserve and most of the European banking industry. The World Bank operates under the authority of the Board of Governors. Each of the institution's 180–member countries is represented by one governor, who is usually a ministerial–level government official. General operation of the Bank is delegated to a smaller group of representatives, the Board of Executive Directors, with the president of the Bank serving as chairman of the board. These executive directors are based in Washington, DC. The Board of Executives Directors is responsible for policy decisions affecting the World Bank's operations and for the approval of all loans. Presently the Bank has 24 executive directors. According to the Articles of Agreement, the five largest shareholders each appoint one executive director; these are France, Germany, Japan, the United Kingdom and the United States. The other countries are grouped into constituencies, each represented by an executive director who is elected by a country or group of countries. The members themselves decide how they will be grouped. Although the World Bank is ostensibly a part of the United Nations, the Bank is accountable solely to its own members and has its own sources of finance, including subscriptions and income from loans. Most of its past presidents come from the same banking houses we have discussed extensively throughout this book. A few brief biographies of past presidents tells us who actually is actually running things.

Lewis T. Preston Term: September 1991 to May 1995. He joined J. P. Morgan & Co. in 1951, where he became President and later Chairman of the Board and CEO, posts he relinquished in 1989. He was Chairman of the Executive Committee of J. P. Morgan from 1989 to February 1991. He served for four years.

Eugene Black (1898–1992). Term: July 1949 to December 1962. He was an investment banker and senior vice president of Chase Manhattan Bank; previously he had been US Executive Director to the Bank and Assistant Secretary at the US Treasury. He served for 13 1/2 years—the longest of any World Bank president.

John J. McCloy (1896–1989). Term: March 1947 to April 1949. He was a lawyer, and his law firm was counsel to Chase National Bank. He held positions in the executive branch of the US government (including Assistant Secretary of War). He resigned from the Bank to become US High Commissioner to Germany.

A. W. Clausen (1923–). Term: July 1981 to June 1986. He was with Bank of America and BankAmerica Corp. for 32 years, serving the last 11 years as President and CEO before coming to the Bank. He returned to BankAmerica Corp. as chairman in 1986. He served for five years.

These are a lot of familiar names: Chase Manhattan [Rockefeller] J. P. Morgan, BankAmerica. And then, there is the current World Bank President, James D. Wolfhenston. His bio is, to quote Yogi Berra, just like deja vu all over again.

> He was Executive Partner of Salomon Brothers in New York and head of its investment banking department. He was Executive Deputy Chairman and Managing Director of Schroders, Ltd., in London, President of J. Henry Schroders Banking Corporation in New York, and Managing Director, Darling & Co. of Australia.

> Schroeder's Bank was, as you recall, the firm that financed Hitler's rise to power. It was represented by the Dulles brothers, John Foster and Allan, future Secretary of State and CIA director, respectively.

The IMF (International Monetary Fund) is owned by the World Bank in the same way that the Federal Reserve is owned by the individual banks we have already looked at. It's all done through a series of interlocking directorates. As one climbs up the ladder, the number of banks involved begin to thin, and the names all begin to sound alike. In the final analysis, the World Bank and the International Monetary Fund are merely international versions of the same European–American banking houses that have dictated international policy for much of the past century.

ELIMINATING THE COMPETITION

In return for massive bailouts, the major global banks are demanding the closure of what is, after all, the only competition. Every country that has refused to this point has suffered the consequences. Economists can confuse the issue using all kinds of fancy terms that don't really make any sense, but the bottom line remains the same. Eliminate the competition, or else. Nobody is arguing that the banks in question made bad loans. But banks are institutions. They can't do anything. Only the people that run them can make decisions. If the true plan was to eliminate the problem, then why not just fire the people that made the bad loans? Liquidating the competition only consolidates the power to lend money in the hands of a smaller and more select group of banks. The fewer banks there are, the less competitive they have to be. That means they can charge whatever interest rates they want. Add whatever fees they want. Where else can you go if they are the only game in town? Of course, on a global scale it's more complicated than that. It isn't the guy on the street that they cater to. Instead, they cater to entire nations. But the principle remains the same. The IMF and the World Bank are dictating the following terms and in a not very subtle manner. The terms are simple. It's my way or the highway. Those who chose the highway found it was a very bumpy road indeed.

MEGA BANKS!

On April 6, 1998, Traveler's Group and Citicorp merged into a giant financial consortium in a deal worth in excess of $76 billion. That merger effectively created the world's largest bank. The new "Traveler's Group" boasted assests of nearly three quarters of a trillion dollars.

A week later, BancOne and First Chicago NBD merged in a $30 billion deal. The same day, NationBank and BankAmerica did the same. In an article entitled "The First

Law of Godzilla—Size Does Matter," *TIME* Magazine said, "On the same day last week that the BankAmerica–NationsBank deal was announced, BancOne chairman John B. McCoy (who once mused that the future the industry would have just five or six major banks) announced plans to merge his $116 billion bank with the much merged $115 billion First Chicago NBC Corp."

McCoy is correct, as we have already pointed out. Five or six mega banks are much easier to control than dozens of smaller ones. And that provides a measure of control over the economy that goes far beyond wealth and well into the sphere of raw, unchecked power. Consider this. The five largest banks in the United States have combined assests of approximately $2.1 trillion! When you consider that the United States is $5.5 trillion in debt, you get some measure of just how much power that actually is!

IIt is the equivalent of having the lifeboat seating concession on the Titanic. Incidentally, those five banks? Well we've met them in various historical incarnations throughout this book. They are, in order, CitiCorp–Traveler's, NationsBank–BankAmerica, Chase Manhattan, JP Morgan and BancOne–First Chicago. All are daughter corporations of the banking royalty of London

THE POLITICS OF THE BAILOUT

Over the past several decades, the rules of the game have shifted, but not too subtly. Still, the shift in strategy still points in the same direction. Prior to World War II, all the power emanated from those who had the money to lend to governments so they could make war. The trick was to create opposing sides to fight with each other. That wasn't a very complicated trick, provided you controlled the purse strings in all countries involved. We've seen how that was accomplished in World War I via the Warburg connections. In World War II, the same principles applied, except the lead bankers involved were of the next generation, with somewhat less recognizable connections. After World War II, the Nuclear Age made war unthinkable. So the Cold War was developed, the balance of power carefully maintained, and the politics of peace became an even greater cash cow than the money lenders could have even imagined. Now, with the end of the Cold War, it is time to start calling in all those markers. The money that was lent to maintain peace is coming due, and the countries that owe it can't pay. Now it's time for the coup de gras—the bailout. As a condition of lending even more money, the upstart banks must die—just as they did in America during the Great Depression. Then the power grab will be complete and absolute. Sounds insidious, doesn't it? But it works.

AND HERE'S HOW

As Indonesia's economy unravelled, food riots there gave the rest of the world a glimpse of what economic meltdown really means. The International Monetary Fund stepped in to bail out the troubled economy. But the IMF demanded certain concessions in return, one of which was that Jakarta allow its troubled rupiah to float instead of being pegged to the US dollar. The president of the Indonesia Central Bank agreed. President Suharto disagreed. Suharto wanted to implement a currency board system that would fix the rupiah's exchange rate with the dollar. The Indonesian currency has plummeted in value in the past seven months while unemployment and inflation have soared. Hundreds of companies face bankruptcy because of huge debts. So Suharto fired his central banker and replaced him with someone a little easier to get along with. Remember, while all this is going on, there are food riots taking place in the streets! The IMF committed $43 billion to the bailout plan, but has held up the check. Suharto has been playing economic chicken with the IMF since the debacle began in August 1997. The IMF wants to control Indonesian banking. Suharto says it infringes on Indonesian sovereignty. The banks behind the bailout are worried their plans may be set back. "Indonesia has a program in place," an IMF official told reporters. He said many areas of the bailout plan would be called into question under a currency board.

"Monetary policy, bank restructuring, interest rates . . . If you put in a currency board, all of this would be affected." In other words, Indonesia's national economic policy would be regulated according to Indonesia's interests, rather than being regulated according to international banking profit margins.

The standoff between Jakarta and the International Monetary Fund could reach far beyond Indonesia's borders. The ripple effect of a total Indonesian meltdown would have global implications. If Indonesia, for example, falls into chaos, we will pay for it with decades of Southeast Asian instability. Similarly, democracy in Thailand will be threatened if IMF conditions there are not eased. The international financial structure is in urgent need of revision, before one of the crises it now generates turns into a global collapse. This will be the litmus test of the IMF's new bail–out policy. If it works, the precedent established by the plan will create a kind of international economic dictatorship against whom no nation will be able to stand.

If it doesn't, there are other plans in the works. In an interview with *Business Week,* Henry Kaufman of the Kaufman Investment Fund, explained:

> "My view is that there ought to be another official institution put in place that is going to monitor and supervise major financial institutions and major markets around the world. The reason that I proposed this back in the 1980s is because of the extraordinary changes in the financial markets."

We've moved to a more securitized market where there are rapid flows of money, where there are intricate trading mechanisms, financing techniques of all sorts. This requires more uniform reporting, more uniform accounting standards, more uniform trading standards, more uniform capital standards. And it requires that they be instituted globally, not just within the US.

LET THE (BLUE) CHIPS FALL WHERE THEY MAY

The ring of fire continued to melt down Asian markets, until it even began to threaten Red China's newly acquired economic interests in Hong Kong. The rout in Hong Kong started when international foreign exchange markets finished cleaning out other Asian countries such as Thailand and Taiwan and set their sights on the Hong Kong dollar. In a move to support its currency, Hong Kong began aggressively selling US dollars and buying Hong Kong dollars. It cut off a cheap source of credit for banks. It also raised interest on overnight loans between banks by 300%, sparking fears that the banks would raise their prime lending rates, undermining Hong Kong businesses and the real

estate market. The crash was the most serious crisis yet for
Hong Kong's new post–colonial rulers. Hong Kong's new
Chinese leader, Tung Chee–hwa, faced his first major crisis
since taking charge in July. The Chinese leader vowed to do
whatever it takes to defend the Hong Kong dollar. That was
precisely what the global planners wanted to hear. As if by
magic, the situation stabilized. There were reverberations
felt around the world, as we shall see, but they were after-
shocks; the main earthquake in Asia had done all the damage that was necessary.

CHAPTER EIGHT

. . .

WALL STREET

"It is quite conceivable that

a few years hence we will look back at this episode,

as we now look back at the 1987 crash,

as a salutary event."

FED CHAIRMAN ALAN GREENSPAN,
COMMENTING ON OCTOBER 27, 1997, STOCK MARKET CRASH

For much of the preceding chapters, we have attempted to explain money as a concept, money as a matter of historical record, money as a tool, and money as power. Even with all that, explaining just what money is requires more. In our world today, money is one of the fundamental principles of our social organization. The cash in one's pocket represents a tiny percentage of the average person's wealth. Most people's homes are financed liabilities—the asset being the equity, or the difference between the property's market value and the dollar amount of the unpaid portion of the property's mortgage. Ownership of property—our individual substance—is represented through monetary claims. In today's society, the real measure of wealth is the degree of ownership one has in the global market place. That is measured in dollar amounts, but is represented by stocks. In a global economy largely financed through bookkeeping entries made on a bank's computer, the principal way of exchanging those monetary claims—or stocks, is in the stock market. Stock wealth is "paper money"—tokens of indebtedness to the stockholder issued by the recipient of the money invested. For example, a share of Microsoft Corporation is an instrument of debt issued by Microsoft to the investor in exchange for the money the stockholder has entrusted to help Bill Gates build his software empire. If Microsoft's earnings go up, so does the value of the debt instrument—the stock certificate that is issued. So, if an investor bought 100 shares of Microsoft for $11 per share in 1977, his "paper" earnings over 20 years would be represented by the selling price of Microsoft stock today (which, by the way, has increased by considerably more than 100 times at the time of this writing). So, in the stock market, an investor who has large stock holdings in companies like Microsoft can be a "paper" millionaire, even though he has only invested a few thousand dollars of his own money and done nothing personally to increase his wealth. The entire value of his substance is directly related to the value of the stock he holds and is 100% dependent on the efforts of the issuing company to maintain or increase the investor's personal wealth. If something happens to cause the stock value to drop, the investor's wealth drops commensurately. This principle was demonstrated most recently on October 27, 1997.

THE 1997 FENDER BENDER

In late October 1997, the Dow Jones plunged a record 554 points. The free fall was widely seen as a precursor to a worldwide stock market crash. Never in history had the stock market taken such a severe beating in a short time. In all, stocks listed on the New York, NASDAQ and American stock exchanges lost $600 billion in a single trading day. What does that actually mean? Nobody can really picture that much money. If you stacked $600 billion into a single stack of $20 bills, it would weigh nearly 28,000 tons! The stack itself would be almost 3000 miles high! At the close, the Dow had fallen some 1,100 points, or 13.3%, from its August 6, 1997, 8259.31 points, ending an unprecedented run of seven years without a correction. What should have been a "crash" was merely a minor fender bender. One day after the greatest point loss in history, the Dow rebounded with the greatest gain in history.

HISTORY FAILS TO REPEAT ITSELF

The previous stock market crashes in 1929 and 1987 were mere blips on the chart compared to the 1997 "correction." By comparison, in 1987, "Black Monday"—stocks fell a whopping 508 points—which represented a decline of more than 22%. But the crash that was predicted did not come. Instead, the next day, stocks rebounded, and more than half the October 27 losses were recovered the following day. What caused such a precipitous calamity? Why didn't the predicted global recession occur? Is the bull market invulnerable?

The end–of–century mergers and acquisition boom, signaled by such megadeals as the $30 billion battle for Washington's MCI Communications Corp., is far broader and deeper than the one that marked the heydays of the roaring '80s.

Wall Street investment bankers say the string of deals is likely to continue, because this boom is about building corporate empires rather than about tearing them apart.

WHAT'S THE PLAN?

The reasons behind the rush to combine are many and vary by industry, but primarily reflect the deregulation of large industries with too many players and the availability of relatively inexpensive capital in the form of corporate stock trading at high values and modest interest rates. Not too dissimilar to the situation just before the Crash of '29, when there were just too many independent banks all cutting themselves in for a slice of the pie. Not only was that unprofitable at the top levels, but it is much more difficult to control an entire industry with so many mavericks who are less easily herded. Add to that the confidence held by many chief executives, whose companies have recently prospered after weathering years of reengineering. Now the payoff is coming in tremendous financial flexibility and the willingness to again focus on growth rather than downsizing.

WHOSE MONEY IS BEHIND IT ALL?

The individual investor is unwittingly behind this latest merger trend. Mutual fund shareholders, who dumped $19 billion a month into equity funds in 1997, according to the Investment Company Institute, now expect outsize investment returns. Indirectly, this puts pressure on money managers and securities analysts to push corporate managers to deliver growth that is far above that which their underlying businesses have been providing. Industries like domestic banking, insurance and utilities, purchase the growth by buying up the competition. "Wall Street cries for earnings and one way to feed the Street is to acquire your way into increased earnings," said John Hughes, a mergers partner in the Washington office of Brown & Wood, a New York law firm.

FROM THE OVAL OFFICE...

But the deal making is about more than satisfying securities analysts. A procession of White House occupants, dating to Jimmy Carter, have supported the deregulation of many of the nation's largest and most basic industries, such as airlines in the 1970s and telecommunications and electric power in the 1990s. Behind this is the international investment banking powers, who anticipate acquiring many of these former monopolies as a way of consolidating their power. The influence of the global economic planners at the highest levels of government becomes more open as the plan comes together. There is an ingenious strategy at work here, that of hiding in plain sight.

PARTNERS IN FACT...

In addition, there is a blurring of the distinctions between what is economically sound and what constitutes an "issue of national security." This is not too difficult a distinction to blend. Obviously, what affects the security of a country is by definition an "issue of national security," whether it is economic, social or military in context. The economic melt-down in the Far East had serious ramifications on Wall Street. That means it caused ripples that emanated to Pennsylvania Avenue and beyond to Main Street, USA. The ramifications of the Far East economic downturn justified US intervention in the Indonesian economy following the October 1997 Wall Street correction. This was hardly the first time the administration has linked US security interests with quelling an economic panic. That was the major argu-ment for rescuing Mexico during the 1995 peso crisis, when the United States stepped in with $12 billion in aid.

Mexico, however, was not only about the peso, it was about drugs and illegal immigrants. When the Clinton administra-tion contributed $3 billion to a fund to stabilize Indonesia—and with it the economies of Southeast Asia—it argued that far more than stock market shocks and fluctuating curren-cies were at stake.

What prompted the administration to move, officials say, was fear that the instability that first racked Asia, then sped to markets around the globe, could turn into something more virulent. Economists have been talking about the dampening effects that continued turmoil in the Asian mar-kets—and a slowdown in growth—could have on US exports. That was certainly a concern, administration offi-cials say. But it was the least of the worries. The bigger strategic concerns come in many varieties and cross a number of Washington's bureaucratic boundaries. The immediate objective of the US action, of course, is what the Treasury calls "market contagion"—the odd ways in which a loss of investor confidence in one nation spreads to others. Often that seems irrational. There is no reason that concerns about Indonesia or Thailand, for example, should rock confidence in Brazil. But currency crises have a way of gathering steam. And in this case, the willingness of governments in Asia to devalue their currencies because their neighbor has—making their goods more competitive—has prompted market speculators to suspect that other governments will follow suit lest they be priced out of the export race.[23]

In the process, the World Bank and the IMF accomplished precisely what they had intended—control of the lucrative currency exchange trade in the rich SouthEast Asian markets. The government of the United States put the full weight of its authority as the world's remaining superpower behind the global banking system—because it had to. The decision was political, but it was not based on the will of the people, but rather the will of the international banking community. It was simply that the American people "benefited" from the decision in the same way the victim of a mugging "benefits" from not being shot by the robber. Or, as the *New York Times* explained it:

> "Today the concerns are very different. But Indonesia is now not only a major market for the United States, and a huge producer and consumer of goods for all of Asia, it intersects a critical shipping route for oil."[1]

That helps explain why the US military command for the Pacific, based at Pearl Harbor, has been searching around to beef up its team of regional economic analysts.

---

[23] *New York Times,* November 3, 1997.

And one of the other major concerns arising from the currency crisis, Clinton administration officials say, has been to make sure that Asians know that the United States is engaged in the region's economic stability. No sooner had the troubles began than Japan proposed the creation of a separate Asian stability fund, one that would sidestep the US–influenced International Monetary Fund. Several Asian countries warmed to the idea, especially those that chafe at the conditions that the IMF places on its loans— closing failing banks (sometimes even those tied to a country's politicians), opening markets, breaking up cozy monopolies. All of those conditions were part of the IMF's package for Indonesia, which will provide the country with $15 billion to $18 billion in immediate financing, and another $12 billion to $15 billion in backup financing if the Asian crisis worsens. Deputy Treasury Secretary Lawrence H. Summers frequently calls rescue operations like the IMF's part of **"preventative diplomacy. These are all part of promoting prosperity,"** he says, **"and maintaining stability."**[24]

The IMF's great vision of preventative diplomacy was quite effective. Suharto refused to knuckle under to the demands of the IMF. The IMF retaliated with a kind of economic "carpet bombing" of the Indonesian populace. Within weeks, the ensuing unrest across Indonesia forced Suharto's resignation after 32 years in power. "Power," of course, is relative. Suahrto held his country in an iron grip for a generation. The IMF was able to shake his grip in a matter of weeks. The power of money cannot be understated.

---

[24] *New York Times,* November 3, 1997.

WHAT'S IN A WORD?

When examining the variables in the market, and what may or may not be the result, it is useful to have a full understanding of the terms we hear all the time, but never make any sense of. Inflation, deflation, what's the difference? And what about hyperinflation? What in the world does that mean?

Many of the terms used by various commentators on financial talk shows, or those used in the *Wall Street Journal* or *Forbes,* don't really give us an accurate picture of the possible ramifications of those scenarios, mainly because nobody ever explains exactly what they mean. First, we'll look at the terms as defined in Barron's *Dictionary of Finance and Investment Terms,*[25] and then we'll spend a little time seeing how each impacts the lives of ordinary Americans.

- Inflation: rise in the price of goods and services, as happens when spending increases relative to the supply of goods on the market—in other words, too much money chasing too few goods. Moderate inflation is a common result of economic growth.

- Hyperinflation: with prices rising at 100% a year or more, causes people to lose confidence in the currency and put their assets in hard assets like real estate or gold, which usually retain their value in inflationary times.

- Deflation: decline in the prices of goods and services. Deflation is the reverse of inflation; it

---

[25] *Dictionary of Finance and Investment Terms,* 4th Edition, © 1995, Barron Educational Series.

should not be confused with disinflation, which is a slowing of the rate of price increases. Generally, the economic effects of deflation are the opposite of those produced by inflation, with two notable exceptions. 1) Prices that increase with inflation do not necessarily decrease with deflation—union wage rates, for example. 2) While inflation may or may not stimulate output and employment, marked deflation has always affected both negatively.

Inflation is really just the result of splitting the monetary unit into multiple parts. Earlier, we saw how the goldsmith of old issued more warehouse receipts than were represented by gold on deposit. To put it simply, if there is a sum total of, say, $100 in actual gold on deposit, if there are $110 in outstanding receipts, the actual value of the gold on deposit is reduced by 10%. The reason is, in the event of a "run" on the goldsmith's "bank," that is, if everyone who held receipts demanded payment at the same time, the best the goldsmith could offer would be 90 cents on the dollar. In the case of the United States, the value of a pre–Federal Reserve 1912 dollar is 100 cents. In 1997, a Federal Reserve note for one dollar is worth—in 1912 dollars—about eight cents. That is the effect of inflation on money that isn't backed by gold.

The Federal Reserve policy of manipulating interest rates to control inflation is merely evidence the Federal Reserve is in control of inflation. In the final analysis, inflation is little more than a hidden tax levied against all citizens, to the benefit of the banking consortium who controls the Federal Reserve. The Fed keeps inflation under control by restricting or relaxing the money supply. In boom times, when

there is plenty of money available, companies have no problem financing expansions and hiring workers.

INFLATION, THE STOCK MARKET AND THE PRICE OF VEGETABLES IN BOISE

As employment levels drop, the cost of employees goes up.
After all, when there are plenty of jobs available, workers
are going to seek the ones that pay the highest and offer the
best range of benefits. So companies are forced to raise
wages and seek wider benefit packages in order to attract
the workers they need in order to complete the expansion
plans financed by all that easy money. If packaging raw
vegetables costs more this year because of higher wages,
then the price of raw vegetables will go up even if there is a
bountiful harvest. The packagers have to cut costs in each
direction, so they will squeeze farmers for the lowest possible price. After all, there are plenty of raw vegetables to
choose from in a bumper crop year. Farmers don't make
quite as much from their harvest. Workers make a little
more thanks to increased competition for labor, but they
also have to pay more for packaged raw vegetables.
Meanwhile, the employer, who borrowed money from the
unrestricted money supply that results from lowered interest
rates, has to include the cost of borrowing money into his
budget. Prices increase slightly. The higher wages the workers receive tend to stimulate spending, prompting other sec-
tors of the manufacturing economy to boost production.
Meaning they borrow money to expand, plus interest.
Workers with a little more money in their pocket sink some
of that into the stock market. That money contributes to the
pool of available cash for manufacturing investment. Some
of the interest that is paid back to the manufacturers who

borrow the money to expand goes into that investment pool in the form of dividends for stock holders, with a little off the top for the banking industry at each step of the way.

When the market takes a tumble, like it did in October 1997, the money that vanishes from the economy, like the $600 billion that evaporated on Blue Monday, has to come from somewhere. The question is, where? The banks aren't taking a loss. Neither are the investment brokers that advise, buy and sell stocks for the investor. For the sake of clarity, we'll use as our "investor" the vegetable packer who invested some of his raise that resulted from the increased competition for workers in a full employment market. Are you still with me? So the $600 billion loss is shared across the board with all those small investors. The "raise" evaporates. Fewer people buy packaged raw vegetables. The manufacturer still has to pay back the interest on the loan he got to expand, but now his profit margin is lower due to a drop in demand. So prices go up even higher. Farmers get squeezed a little more. Next year they grow fewer vegetables. The price of seed goes up due to a reduction in demand. Workers get laid off. Everybody loses a little bit—except the money suppliers, who get their cut off the top. Everybody pays, just like taxes, except Congress is bypassed, the national treasury gets smaller instead of bigger, and nobody really knows why their purchasing power is diminished. They just know that it is. In effect, what appears to be rising prices is really a reflection of the lowering of the value of the dollar. That is inflation, and the Federal Reserve takes credit for keeping the economy in check by restricting the money supply to "check inflation." All the while, it's a process they deliberately started in motion!

A DEFLATIONARY TALE

A deflationary spiral is far more dangerous to the economy as a whole than is inflation. Inflation raises prices, which is a concept everybody older than 25 can appreciate. Deflation, on the other hand, reduces prices. That sounds like a good thing, on the surface. Everybody likes to get a price break. The problem is, the reduction in prices is also financed on the back of the overall economy, and the banks still get their cut off the top. Here's a typical deflationary scenario. A crash on Wall Street causes businesses to lose all their capital. The businesses are stuck with a lot of excess inventory and no cash. To raise cash to liquidate their debts, they sell off inventory at below cost to the public. The public, eager to cash in on the lower prices, spend their savings on things they wouldn't ordinarily buy. Meanwhile, the businesses are unable to meet payroll, forcing worker layoffs. The laid–off workers can't afford to buy from business, even though prices are going down all the time. Credit is restricted by the banks because the business down cycle makes lending too risky. Failed businesses don't pay taxes, neither do laid off workers. The government's operating capital is reduced accordingly. A reduction in the tax base forces a reduction in the federal work force and a reduction in government services. That further reduces the consumer base and the tax base. Businesses cut prices further, hoping to obtain at least some cash from their excess inventory. But nobody has any money to buy. Soon, if a new car is selling for $1,000—it's a bargain, except that nobody has $1,000. The car sits rusting on the lot, a liability now, instead of an asset. The only guy in town who still has a job is the guy who makes sure nobody steals it. As the cycle continues, more businesses fail for lack of cash, more workers are thrown out of work, the value of goods decline, real estate prices depress, and the country is in the throes of a deflationary spiral. Meanwhile, those who control the money supply are "stuck" with property, businesses and assets that they were "forced" to foreclose on when the loans went into default. They, in turn, sell that property for pennies on the dollar to those few super wealthy whose cash was not in the market on the fateful day. "Paper" millionaires are selling apples on street corners, while the genuine millionaires emerge on the other side of the business cycle as billionaires. That last such period of deflation was set in motion by the stock market crash of 1929, which was the direct cause of the Great Depression.

NOT EVERYBODY TAKES A BEATING

As in previous crashes, only the lemmings take a real beating. The smart money knows when to hold 'em, and when to fold 'em. In America, as elsewhere, the rich get richer, on a selective basis, according to the future plans of the money manipulators. Remember, the power behind the throne is wealth— and that wealth may, for a time, be concentrated in the hands of a few. The power to manipulate that wealth puts those select few in the hands of those who are able to maintain the lifestyles of the rich and famous. During the Depression, it was the Rockefellers, Morgans, Mellons and Carnegies who were able to emerge from the ashes as billionaires whose wealth was now distributed through various tax–free foundations serving the globalist aims. The ownership of that wealth was buried under a series of interlocking directorates, but the power remained concentrated in the hands of those who controlled the directorates. A look at the latest "crash" demonstrates that principle. How did the fabulously wealthy "owners" of the global establishment fare in 1997?

The five richest Americans, according to the most recent ranking by Forbes magazine, saw the value of their principal holdings shrink by nearly $4 billion. But the losses were only paper losses, designed to prove that nobody was invulnerable. Earlier in the year, massive amounts of money quietly moved out of the "danger zone"—$3.5 billion in July, $4 billion in August, $4.5 billion in September—and into "safe havens" designed to maintain the concentration of economic power after the crash. Before the next trading day was over, those same "victims" whose $4 billion in losses made headlines had recovered $3.6 billion of their money back. The lucky few?

- Bill Gates, chairman and chief executive of Microsoft Corp.
- Warren Buffett, chairman and CEO of Berkshire Hathaway Inc.
- Paul Allen, co–founder of Microsoft Corp.
- Larry Ellison, chairman, CEO and president of Oracle Corp.
- Gordon Moore, chairman of Intel Corp.
- Michael Dell, chairman and CEO of Dell Computer Corp.
- Walton family, Wal–Mart Inc.
- Phil Knight, chairman and CEO of Nike Inc.
- Ted Turner, vice chairman of Time Warner Inc.

Note that five of the above control computer empires are essential to the continued operation of the global economy.

Two are global retailing giants with immense holdings in the "melted down" Asian markets, and, of course, Ted Turner. Turner is an avid globalist who had earlier in the year donated some $1 billion to the United Nations. Turner controls the largest news organization on the face of the planet—CNN/*Headline News,* and recently merged his organization with the media giant *TIME*/Warner. Turner once (accurately) bragged that CNN had more to do with the collapse of Communism than Ronald Reagan. Others may come and go, but these men, especially Bill Gates and Ted Turner, are as necessary for maintaining the global economic status quo as John D. Rockefeller and Paul Warburg were to the maintaining of the Federal Reserve banking system during the Great Depression.

CHAPTER NINE

MORTGAGING THE HOMESTEAD

"This is a budget only a liberal could love.

We cannot afford to return to the old days

of high taxes, more spending and a larger,

less accountable government."

HOUSE SPEAKER NEWT GINGRICH
ON THE 1999 FEDERAL BUDGET

DEFICIT, DEBT— WHAT'S THE DIFFERENCE?

One of the least understood mechanisms of the global economic machine is the concept of the American national debt. To many people, the budget deficit and the national debt are interchangeable terms. That is not so—in fact, they are not even close! The budget deficit is the difference between what it costs to operate government and provide government services and the amount of money actually in the national checkbook. Although it's a little more complicated than this, think of the budget deficit as a kind of overdraft protection. Each Federal Reserve note is really a check written on the United States' checking account. If there are more checks outstanding than the money in the account, then once all the checks are presented for payment, the checking account is overdrawn. In other words, the US government deficit is really just a way of expressing the number of bounced checks the US has outstanding. The banks that stand behind the Federal Reserve system guarantee overdraft protection. If more checks are presented for payment than the government can actually redeem, the Federal Reserve "loans" the Treasury the difference with interest.

THE WAY DEFICIT SPENDING WORKS

Consider your own checking account. Suppose you have arranged a $2,000 overdraft protection with your bank. You have a balance of $750 but you write a check for a new TV for $1,500. The amount of cash you have is $750. The other $750 is protected by your overdraft. The additional $750 you don't have is what the government calls "deficit spending." The amount of interest the bank charges you on the overdraft amount continues to compound until you put back the $750 into your account that you have technically borrowed by going into your overdraft. That $750 is debt. You can leave it outstanding for as long as you wish, and every month the amount will grow as the interest is deducted from the money you actually do have. Eventually, your debt which resulted from your deficit spending will grow to $800, or $900, or, $1,000, and, left long enough, it could go to $2,000. Because your overdraft is limited to $2,000, once you reach that point, every check you write will bounce. Assuming your debt plus interest reaches $2,000, you would have to make a $2,000 deposit to your checking account to bring the balance up to $0. If you were to deposit $3,000 into your checking account, you could then say you had a surplus of $1,000 and no debt. That is different from what the government calls a budget surplus. In government doublespeak, a budget surplus is when you have limited out your overdraft but don't get it extended. You still owe the amount you borrowed, plus the accumulated interest. And the interest continues to accumulate on the money outstanding in your overdraft account, day after day, week after week. Balancing the budget does not mean you've paid off your overdraft. It just means you aren't making it any larger by spending. It still continues to grow because your banker is charging you interest on the money you already owe. It's a little like rolling over your mortgage every year to pay off your outstanding utility bills. The problem is this. Every year, the mortgage principal gets higher, instead of lower. The payments go up as interest is added, and so the debt grows instead of shrinks. The interest on the larger amount grows exponentially. Each year you fall further behind, and the payments take a bigger chunk of your paycheck. To keep up, you have to spend more than you make, and roll over the difference into your next mortgage. Which means next year's mortgage takes an even bigger chunk. If you get a raise, you have slightly more money available to spend, so the amount you overspend, based on your current debt, goes down slightly. Notice, you haven't reduced your debt by a single cent; instead, it continues to go up based on the escalating interest alone. Reducing your deficit merely slows the rate at which you reach total insolvency. The process itself is inexorable. Unless your pay raise is enough to pay off your existing mortgage, interest and all, and leaves you with enough capital to meet next year's bills, you'll never make it to a "break even" point. Never! Reducing the deficit, as the term is bandied about in public, really means we have slowed the rate at which we are drowning. In the case of the United States National Debt, balancing the budget might forestall the day in which our debt reaches critical mass by a year or two, but not much more.

THE NATIONAL DEBT

"I place economy among the first and most important virtues, and public debts among the greatest of dangers. To preserve our independence, we must not let our rulers load us with perpetual debt."

THOMAS JEFFERSON

The current national debt figure is so enormous as to be mind numbing. It is currently more than $5.4 trillion and increasing at the rate of $613 million per day. The following chart shows just how fast our economic vitality is being drained.[26]

---

[26] Source: Bureau of the Public Debt.

BY MONTH—1997

10/31/1997 . . . . $5,427,225,185,059.66
09/30/1997 . . . . $5,413,146,011,397.34
08/29/1997 . . . . $5,404,420,294,885.51
07/31/1997 . . . . $5,373,228,560,474.27
06/30/1997 . . . . $5,376,151,252,876.02
05/30/1997 . . . . $5,344,961,362,266.83
04/30/1997 . . . . $5,353,971,314,439.39
03/31/1997 . . . . $5,380,889,857,391.59
02/28/1997 . . . . $5,349,937,360,942.68
01/31/1997 . . . . $5,313,997,018,848.05
12/31/1996 . . . . $5,323,171,750,783.19
11/29/1996 . . . . $5,296,548,923,143.63

BY YEAR—FISCAL YEAR
ENDING SEPTEMBER 30

09/30/1997 . . . . $5,413,146,011,397.34
09/30/1996 . . . . $5,224,810,939,135.73
09/29/1995 . . . . $4,973,982,900,709.39
09/30/1994 . . . . $4,692,749,910,013.32
09/30/1993 . . . . $4,411,488,883,139.38
09/30/1992 . . . . $4,064,620,655,521.66
09/30/1991 . . . . $3,665,303,351,697.03
09/28/1990 . . . . $3,233,313,451,777.25
09/29/1989 . . . . $2,857,430,960,187.32
09/30/1988 . . . . $2,602,337,712,041.16
09/30/1987 . . . . $2,350,276,890,953.00

HOW DID WE LET THIS HAPPEN?

Until the 1930s the government was pretty much solvent. To be sure, there was some public debt incurred during war time. We've already looked at the war debt mechanism in some detail. But when times got tough during the Depression, the people cried out to the government to help them. That was all the banking cartel needed to hear. President Franklin D. Roosevelt was just the man to put the plan into action. Along came the various public projects— the WPA, TVA, CCC, and a host of other projects that pretty much exhausted the public employees charged with coming up with easy–to–remember acronyms to identify them. There are already many excellent books detailing the various public works enterprises that were created as the forerunners of entitlements, so we won't spend a lot more time looking at the details. It was during this period that Social Security was born (more on its role later). Welfare made the transformation from private charity to public responsibility. The concept of perpetual debt entered into the American consciousness. The transformation of the American mind was gradual; first these programs were but a small part of the overall budget. Over the years, people came to expect government hand outs, after a time, they began to demand them. President Lyndon Johnson's "War on Poverty" (The Great Society) accelerated the growth of the public debt as he attempted to rewrite history by being the first leader to successfully fight a two–front war. Johnson introduced Medicare, Medicaid, and a host of other programs that didn't seem to be all that expensive, at the time. But nobody was paying attention to the Big Picture. On the home front, Johnson waged war on poverty, while simultaneously attempting to finance the war in Vietnam. The financiers who were supplying the money just kept writing checks, as the United States Treasury kept signing IOU's. The US surrendered the gold standard; in 1969, we surrendered the silver standard and scrapped our silver coins. Presidents Nixon and Ford passed the debt along to the next generation, borrowing to pay for their political patronage along the way. By the time President Carter took office, the debt was so enormous relative to the US GDP that interest rates were hovering near 20% and the worst business cycle downturn since the Depression had America in despair. President Reagan was elected in 1978 on a promise to redesign the economy. He did so, but unfortunately, built his economic platform on the earnings of the generation of Americans yet to be born. The budget deficit skyrocketed, but America was living high for the first time in a decade, and nobody gave much thought to how, or who, was going to pay the bill when it came. Between 1980 and 1990, the National Debt increased 400%. At the time, those who expressed their concern were stifled by the economists who pontificated loudly about how "we were just borrowing from ourselves anyway." The fact is, as we have already seen, we didn't borrow it from ourselves; we sold it to the United Kingdom, Hong Kong (now Red China) and to the Japanese. They hold, respectively, the three largest concentrations of our national bad paper. The remaining debt is made up of outstanding Treasury bills, savings bonds and other instruments of indebtedness that are regularly sold at public auction. Every time the government needs more, they just ask the Fed to issue more securities. This mortgaging of the national homestead to live now and pay later is the reason the United States concurrently occupies the roles of both the world's largest debtor nation and the world's wealthiest nation.

The combination of these two opposing national characteristics makes America extremely vulnerable to those who write the checks. There is a price to be paid, now, and in the future.

THE GULF WAR AND THE BANK DICK

There was a classic movie from the 1930s called *The Bank Dick* that cast W. C. Fields as an inept bank guard in a small–town bank. Field's character wanted to do well, and it was obvious he hated working for the bank, whose president harangued him unmercifully. But the Bank Dick just couldn't break out of his rut. He had this little problem, which he kept in a flask in his pocket. . . .

In this old movie, we can find a parallel between America's relationship with the global economic leadership and W. C. Fields' classic 1930s character. America is the world's bank guard—not necessarily by choice, but rather, because of the flask it keeps in its pocket. W. C. Fields kept liquor in his flask; America keeps oil in hers.

MY LITTLE CHICKADEE

In the months leading up to the Gulf War, Iraq swept into Kuwait, seizing a significant percentage of the world's oil reserves. CIA officials were in possession of information that his battle plan called for consolidating his position there before moving against the oil–rich kingdom of Saudi Arabia. From the various pulpits in Congress, the UN and the Oval Office, President George Bush proclaimed a "new world order" in which he pledged the United States to be the protector of democratic principles wherever they might be threatened. That included, especially, the President said, Kuwait and Saudi Arabia. No one questioned the obvious. What democratic principles? Kuwait was and is a kingdom with no discernible democratic principles whatsoever. Saudi Arabia is a theocracy which, at best, was and is a benevolent dictatorship. Both nations had no desire or interest in democracy, had no love for the United States or its political system, and bore a deep and abiding distrust bordering on hatred for Western culture in general. What they did have was oil. Most of the world's oil supply is still controlled by the Standard Oil Trust, a Rockefeller property. The UN coalition against Iraq had the full backing of the Rockefeller Foundation and its many offspring. Both Secretary of State George Schultz and Secretary of Defense Caspar Weinberger were officials of the Bechtel Corporation—the world's largest construction conglomerate, which also happens to be owned by the Rockefeller family. George Schultz was a Rockefeller heir. The UN headquarters in New York was donated by John D. Rockefeller. The Rockefeller Chase Manhattan Bank is the only corporate entity in the world to have its own UN envoy.

That's not to say the US acted solely to protect the interests of the Rockefeller family. But it is closer to the truth than is the public rhetoric that the US was going to the Middle East to protect Kuwaiti and Saudi democratic ideals. America was sent to the Gulf to protect its economic interests, and it was sent there by those who controlled America's economic destiny. It was the politics of oil that oversaw the Gulf War coalition against Saddam Hussein, not democratic principles. America's involvement was a direct result of its allegiance to those who hold the national mortgage, part of the interest due on the national debt.

THE SOCIAL SECURITY SYSTEM

The Social Security Administration was created during the 1930s by the Roosevelt Administration. On the surface, it was always promoted as an entitlement in which the recipients had a vested interest as a result of contributions made over the course of a lifetime. In reality, it serves three separate purposes.

First, it provides the legal framework to obligate each individual American for his share of the national debt. The Federal Insurance Contribution Act (FICA) defines "contribution," according to Blackstone's *Law Dictionary:*

> "Contribution. Right of one who has discharged a common liability to recover of another also liable, the aliquot portion which he ought to pay or bear. Under principle of "contribution," a tort–feasor against whom a judgment is rendered is entitled to recover proportional shares of judgment from other joint tort–feasor whose negligence contributed to the injury and who was also liable to the plaintiff (cite omitted). The share of a loss payable by an insurer when contracts with two or more insurers cover the same loss. The insurer's share of a loss under a coinsurance or similar provision. The sharing of a loss or payment among several. The act of any one or several of a number of co–debtors, co–sureties, etc., in reimbursing one of their number who has paid the whole debt or suffered the whole liability, each to the extent of his proportionate share."[27]

---

[27] *Blackstone's Law Dictionary*, 6th Edition.

A COMPLICATED SHELL GAME

Secondly, the Social Security system provides a convenient method for hiding the true state of the national debt and budget deficit/surpluses. By declaring the monies collected under FICA rules as a "trust fund" the government can "borrow" against the trust, replacing it with Treasury bills, which are redeemable upon demand. However, because they are redeemable upon demand, and that the redemption price comes out of the US Treasury itself, that makes T–bills an instrument of debt. So the T–bills used as collateral against loans from the Social Security Trust fund are actually debts that are counted as assets for accounting purposes. When calculating the national debt, therefore, the $1 trillion or so dollars that are supposed to be in trust for Social Security benefits are used to reduce the overall debt picture by that amount. The cash the government "borrows" from the trust turns up in government ledgers as income, reducing the deficit figures while in reality increasing the debt. In other words, the asset of $1 trillion is actually a liability of $1 trillion, thereby reducing the appearance of the national debt by a total of $2 trillion. It's confusing, and deliberately so. Let's cut to a simpler image. Look in your wallet or purse and find a dollar. Put it on the table. Now write yourself a check for one dollar. Spend the dollar in cash. Now count the check as an asset of one dollar. Remember, a check is simply an IOU. Until it is cashed, it is a dollar. Once it is cashed it is a liability. You started with one dollar in cash. In theory, you still have it, even though you've spent it, as long as you don't ever cash the check.

Sometime around 2010, retiring baby boomers will begin cashing the IOU's that currently represent the Social Security "trust." Until then, they buy us the illusion of a balanced budget, supported by hidden government IOU's.

THE CONTROL FACTOR

The third purpose of Social Security is to keep tabs on the government's only real asset—your income. Because a Federal Reserve note isn't backed by gold, silver or tangible assets, it is what is called "fiat money," an instrument of debt backed by the credit of the issuer. In this case, the collateral is the property and income of the co–guarantors of the loan. That would be the citizens of the United States. A federal reserve note is a promise to pay and is only evidence of debt. That means that your income is the property of the United States, under the provisions of the 14th Amendment. In reality, when each of us files our IRS tax forms each year, we are not calculating how much we give the government. The government, via the mechanism Social Security and Blackstone's Law, actually already owns everything we earn in advance. What we calculate when we send in our tax returns is the amount the government gives to us! It's really not that much of a distinction, except as a matter of law. The introduction of the Social Security system includes assigning each tax payer a numbered tracking system that details our earnings, keeps the government informed of our whereabouts, and ensures that we don't abscond with any of its money. Remember, you can't even get a driver's license or open a bank account without your Social Security number, let alone get a job! It's a pretty comprehensive system of control. It also gives the government legitimate collateral to back its debt and its future borrowing.

PAYING OFF THE NATIONAL DEBT

Because all US currency is actually evidence of debt instead of being evidence of wealth, the harsh reality is this. We cannot pay off the national debt. Period. One can't pay a debt with a debt! To assume we can pay off our debt is an equivalent absurdity to believing you can pay off your bank loan by using your credit cards. The debt remains; it merely changes ownership, from the bank to the credit card issuer. That is the situation in America. Where it all falls into place is where we began this examination of our national dilemma. When an individual finds himself so deeply in debt that it is all he can do to maintain his situation, the worm turns. In the beginning, when a borrower applies for a loan, he is the one negotiating from a position of power. At the local level, between individual borrowers and lending institutions, if the borrower doesn't like the terms, he can take his business elsewhere. The bank, credit card issuer, mortgage company or lender competes for his share of the business. That is how it makes a profit. If all the customers go across the street to the competition, the lender is soon out of business, and the various employees are out of a job. They earn their living by lending you money.

But once you sign on the dotted line, the situation reverses. Whatever you pledged for collateral, whether it is your new home, car, or just your good name, it is now in the control of the lender. If you need more time to meet your obligations or if you need more money, it is you who negotiates from a position of weakness, not the lender. If the lender wants your house more than he wants the money you owe him, that is his prerogative. It's up to him, not you. The moment you go into default, he can choose to foreclose, or extend, depending on what is good for him, not you. So much for being in charge of your own destiny. You sold that birthright in exchange for a loan.

THE 1998 BUDGET "SURPLUS"

In early 1998, President Clinton called a press conference to announce "the end of the deficit." On an easel erected for the purpose, the president drew a giant circle, saying it represented the current US budget deficit figure. Immediately, the cry went up across the land, "what will we do with the surplus?" Lobbyists descended on Washington. Politicians started pandering to the special interest groups that elected them almost before the news conference had ended. The Republicans wanted to enact tax cuts. The White House announced plans to "save Social Security first." Not surprisingly, the financial community supported any plan that included spending and discouraged any plan that might reduce the overall national debt and the interest payments on that debt. What makes an interesting footnote is the fact the "surplus" doesn't even exist! It's merely a projected surplus, dependent for its existence upon a number of variables. Sixty–five billion dollars of the surplus is to come from the tobacco settlement deal negotiated between the industry and federal prosecutors. Assuming the courts uphold the deal and the industry pays up on time, in cash, the money will be paid in annual installments over five years. In other words, five years from 1998, the US will see the Surplus of 1998! Spending a projected surplus is just another method of deficit spending, repackaged with a new name but the same result. Unlimited debt, without political accountability.

The "surplus" is also dependent upon continued record performance by the stock market. Provided the next five years see economic growth similar to the previous five years, there is a budget surplus. If the economy fails to perform up to previous standards, then the "surplus" evaporates. Finally, the "surplus" exists only if there are no unforeseen calamities like wars, oil shortages, crop failures or other expensive disasters.

THE UNTOUCHABLES

In our current global economic structure, the United States may have all the bombs, military forces and hardware to bomb Saddam back into the Stone Age, but that cuts no ice with those who hold our mortgage papers. We need credit to maintain our awesome arsenal. That means there are entities that are untouchable, countries, central banks and investors to whom we must go, hat in hand, and treat with kid gloves in order to maintain our standard of living. The number–one holder of our debt is Europe. Like any lender, foreclosure depends on what works best for the one who lends the money. Because, by definition, the national debt cannot be repaid, it will also, by definition, continue to grow. At the point when it exceeds our ability to pay, the ball will be in Europe's court. The decision concerning whether to foreclose will be based entirely on what works for them, not us. And that brings us to our examination of the European situation, its goal, and America's ultimate financial destiny.

CHAPTER TEN

EUROPE'S RACE TOWARD UNIFICATION

"Only a virtuous people

are capable of freedom.

As nations become corrupt and vicious,

they have more need of masters."

BENJAMIN FRANKLIN

GLOBALISM AND RELIGION

In the course of examining the developing global economy, there is an element that can't be ignored. Part of the Christian theological study of the last days includes a provision for a global or one–world economy. According to the Book of the Revelation, the Antichrist will ascend to a position of global leadership. Interestingly, the Book of Daniel indicates his headquarters and power base will be located in Europe. One of the most oft quoted and best known of Biblical prophecies is what is generally referred to as the "mark of the Beast." It isn't the purpose of this book to propagate this worldview, nor to denigrate it, but to merely examine it in the light of what is happening today. According to the Book of the Revelation, the Beast, or Antichrist, will develop a system whereby he will be able to control all commerce. Revelation Chapter 13 says that during his reign, **"no man might buy or sell, save he who has the mark, or the name of the beast, or the number of his name" (Revelation 13:17).** This prophecy, penned nearly 2,000 years ago, fits precisely into the developing global system we see today.

THE POLITICAL SYSTEM

Anybody who hasn't spent the last 20 years in a cave knows that the global political system is becoming increasingly interdependent. Few countries can make independent decisions without taking into account the wishes of the global body politic. Countries like Israel and Iraq are cases in point. Israel is unable to make decisions even about its own internal political preferences, such as the location of its capital city. Although Israel has declared Jerusalem to be its capital, Israel's Embassy Row is still located in Tel Aviv. The United Nations has declared through an unending series of resolutions that Israel has no sovereign control over Jerusalem, despite its long Jewish history and its location in the heart of that nation. Iraq undertook to reclaim what it called its Province 19. Today it is Kuwait, but prior to the redefinition of the map of the Middle East following World War I, it was a province in what was then Mesopotamia. When Iraq attempted to regain control of what was a historical part of its empire, the combined forces of the United Nations launched an attack which devastated Iraq's military force. The global body politic dictated terms under which Iraq could buy or sell, calling them "economic sanctions." At this point, the United Nations serves as something of a benevolent dictatorship, but it isn't hard to imagine the rise of a more authoritarian regime modeled after the UN but with less egalitarian views.

THE EUROPEAN SUPERSTATE

The Biblical prophecies concerning a coming global economic system are astonishingly accurate when observed from the position of hindsight. It's here, so to speak, and in our face. But there is more, all of which fits within our current or immediately foreseeable political and economic scene. Writing some 2500 years ago, the prophet Daniel said that there would be a series of four global empires that would come on the scene and pass from view. He predicted them in order. Historians and religious scholars agree that those empires were Babylon, Medo–Persia, Greece (under Alexander the Great) and Rome. Of these four, Daniel said three would be destroyed. The fourth, Rome, would decay from within, but would again rise to global prominence at a particular point in history. History records the decline of the Roman empire, but the continuing influence of Rome itself continued through the ages to the present time. Beginning with the Benelux Treaty in 1948, the countries of Western Europe began to form an economic and political entity that was codified under a 1957 treaty called the "Treaty of Rome." The Treaty of Rome was the foundational document for the modern European superstate. According to the Biblical prophets, Rome will continue to develop its hegemony until it has regained the power and status it had under the Caesars of old. Whether or not that is happening, and the degree to which it will continue, depends on how you look at it. But it certainly seems to be a reasonable hypothesis, with or without input from the Biblical prophets. Europe is poised to take over the global economy. There can be little doubt of that. It also stands ready to step into the vacuum that will be created if and when the United Nations goes the way of the League of Nations that preceded it. For millions of Christians, the rise of a European superstate, in complete control of the global economy, and headed by a leader who will wield broad dictatorial powers is a foregone conclusion. For those who merely observe trends as they develop, it is extremely interesting. Because regardless of the source of information one might use to extrapolate the probable future, one reaches very similar conclusions. The future of the global economy is undeniably linked to Europe. No matter who says so.

MYTH BECOMES REALITY

According to Greek myth, Europa was born when Zeus, lord of the Olympian gods, transformed himself into a bull and coaxed a Phoenician princess named Europa to climb on his back. When Europa mounted, Zeus hurried away to the island of Crete and begat Minos, the first European king. One day, the birth of a unified European nation may inspire a similar tale. Once upon a time, the story will go, Germany, economic powerhouse of the 15 nations of the European Union, transformed itself into a bull and coaxed the other 14 to climb on its back. Then it hurried away to Frankfurt and begat the euro, Europe's single currency.

So far, however, the modern seduction has not gone as well as the classical, and it's no wonder. If the members of the European Union, a federation of states founded in 1957, really do decide to jump on Germany's back and adopt a single currency, their sacrifice will be enormous. They will surrender the right to independently balance their own budgets and manage their own debts. They will relinquish an individual monetary identity. The French franc, the British pound and the Spanish peseta will all cease to exist. The new currency notes are slated to appear in July 2002. The conversion from the many currencies to one—and the transfer of economic management from state central banks to a single European Central Bank—will set interest rates for all. In theory, when the economic efforts of 370 million people are combined this way, European goods and services will be better represented in the world economy by an overarching institution capable of maintaining price stability in all member countries at home and a single stable currency abroad. As it is, European levels of inflation vary wildly, and currencies often seem at war with one another. In the new Europe, the European Central Bank will be seated in the German financial capital of Frankfurt and modeled on the German Central Bank. The symbolism infuriated the French government, which thinks it should be the model for all things European. In order for monetary union to work, all nations must bring annual budget deficits under 3% of GDP and overall national debt below 60% of GDP. In addition, strict inflation and interest rate targets also have to be met. Germany has insisted on the tough conditions to ensure that it does not come out the loser in abandoning its strong deutsche mark. On the other hand, the French complain that Germany itself does not even meet the standards. "When you're in a community, you have to try to reach a consensus rather than imposing your point of view," the French government complains, largely because it has been unable to impose the French point of view. More than a trade surplus is at stake. The effort to meet the membership criteria is already dictating major social—and economic—policy decisions in several countries. Once in the monetary union, nations would face penalties and fines if their budget deficits grew beyond target levels. And with a "no bailout" pledge from members, countries could in theory even go bankrupt if their local economies fail while the central bank kept money tight. Then there is the symbolic question of national identity.

WHOSE EUROPE WILL IT BE?

Two world wars have been fought this century in an effort to unify Europe by force. In both instances, the aggressor was defeated because of the strong sense of identity among the conquered nations. This is not a small thing. Britain claims it will hold off joining the monetary union on nationalistic grounds. This will have the effect of forestalling full union in Europe until the time is right for the banks to consolidate their holdings in advance. Eurocash is expected to have a blank space for "national" symbols to be added by each country. This is part of the advance planning necessary to ensure that the banking cartel's control of the currency is perceived to be a domestic issue, instead of being international. The same principle was involved in creating the Federal Reserve and naming it "federal," which it isn't, and "reserve," which is also incorrect. But it creates the impression that it is a government institution with reserves on hand. The new "national" Euro currency is designed to accomplish a similar deception.

TARGET 1999

Barring unforeseen changes, the euro will become official as of New Year's Day 1999. From that moment on, countries that meet the criteria will have the option of paying their debts in euros. Companies will be able to make transfers in euros. Most complicated financial transactions will take place in the new currency.

The exchange rate of participating countries' currencies will be locked in—against one another and against the euro—from that day on.

THE CARROT AND THE STICK

The United Kingdom has been the major holdout to what would otherwise be a relatively easy and quick economic merger of Europe. After months of waffling, Britain's new government announced in mid–1997 that it was dropping its objections to economic union. Almost immediately, major European corporations began announcing merger plans with other European corporations located in different economic zones. French companies bought Italian companies, German companies merged with companies in France, Italy,

Spain and Portugal. These mergers had been unthinkable earlier, because the rates of exchange between European nations fluctuate wildly. What might be a great deal for an Italian automobile manufacturer this week could, because of an unfavorable exchange rate, be the ruination of a German corporation whose investment capital could evaporate, should the currency rates change before all the paperwork was completed. So, until the British announcement, corporations were hesitant to engage in cross–border investment. Britain's reversal of policy was like pulling a plug out of a dam. Billions of lira, marks, francs and pounds began criss-crossing European borders as if they were already erased.

THE BATTLE STRATEGY

For years, major banks in Germany, like Dresdner Bank and Deutsche Bank, have had their eye on French banks and insurance companies varying from Paribas SA to Societe Generale SA, the Banque Nationale de Paris SA, Groupe des Assurances Nationales SA and Credit Commercial de France SA, but the French companies were reluctant to risk the loss represented by currency fluctuations between the two countries. As the reality of a single currency approaches, European financial services companies are rushing to make themselves large enough to meet the coming competition. French banks and insurers have lagged behind many of their European rivals in getting ready. They just needed a little push, reasoned the money monopoly on Fleet Street, and the assurance that Britain would lift its objections to monetary union was just what the doctor ordered. Business mergers are a little like military conquests. Merger battles are waged on a number of different fronts at once. The principal weapon is money. Each side of a takeover wants to be assured it will end up with more money than it started with. Meanwhile, there are spy vs. spy games taking place behind closed doors, in the boardrooms, in the meeting rooms, and at the highest levels of government. As in war, the ultimate goal is the acquisition of the property. The more you control, the greater the power. A large empire, organized into smaller organizations, each taking orders from above, is much easier to control than dozens of small, independent organizations. The European market place is the next emerging global superpower. In every financial organization, there is a plan. The plan is not necessarily presented for public consumption; sometimes that can work against the common good. Europe is an organization of independent states who have banded together for economic reasons. Where you have an organization, you have planners, and where you have planners, you have people positioned to carry out the plan. Not too illogical, is it?

For the plan to enjoy any chance of success, a certain degree of centralization is necessary. Corporate mergers across borders is part of that centralization plan. But it has to move in steps.

CENTRALIZATION STEP ONE

It is interesting to note that the wave of mergers in 1997 are, in the main, among competing financial institutions across Europe. As in the US during the panics of the 19th century, and the coup de gras—the Crash of 1929 and the subsequent Depression—smaller financial institutions must be either absorbed or eliminated in order to reduce the number of independents. That is the key to control. But it must be selective, and there must be a way to put on the brakes.

That is where the United Kingdom fits in. As we have already seen, the Fleet Street stock exchange has been centralized under the control of the Rothschild banking groups since 1815 or so. The lion's share of the United States' national debt is concentrated in British hands, and the future of European economic union rises or falls based on the UK's willingness to join the economic family. There are economists and European politicians who loudly proclaim "Who needs them?" But those are just words. As the saying goes, talk is cheap. If you want to know how much influence the UK has over Europe's future economic viability, all you need to do is watch.

IT'S NOT YOUR FATHER'S CHRYSLER ANYMORE

The wave of corporate mergers hasn't crested yet. Recently, Daimler–Benz AG of Germany announced plans to buy Chrysler Corp for $38 billion. Over the past four months dozens of banks and industrial giants in the US have been swallowed by parent banks or become part of a European multinational corporate structure. The deals have been worth $114 billion. As of May, 1998, it's a new record.

It isn't just American companies that are becoming part of the larger European conglomerate. Daimler also has a deal in the works with Nissan Motor Company of Japan. A Nissan official confirmed that the company has been looking for a buyer for its commercial truck operation, which also would include its diesel division. Daimler is rushing to develop direct–injection diesel engines, which are highly fuel–efficient and burn cleaner than current models. The company plans to use the engines in light trucks, such as sport–utility vehicles, that are made at its Alabama plant. If the Chrysler acquisition is approved, the engines also could be used in Chrysler sport–utility vehicles. Europe is consolidating its strength politically and economically through its single currency. European corporations are doing the same through corporate takeovers. Now, all these mergers are fueled by a rising stock market. That enables companies to use their own shares as currency to buy other companies. Entire corporations are being bought and sold using phantom money. The list of competitors is shrinking fast.

The recent burst of deals comes in the midst of a record merger spree that began in 1995. The rate of big deals has accelerated in the past year due to high flying stock prices, confidence in the state of the economy and the notion that companies need mass to compete in a global marketplace. At least, that's the argument. But there is another reality to consider. Pretty soon all the marbles will be in the hands of those select few banking and industrial families at the top. And all the power that comes with it.

SORRY, JUST KIDDING

On October 28, 1997, three weeks after Britain announced it would drop objections, and after the planned wave of cross border acquisitions were accomplished, Britain announced a stunning reversal of policy. Under the headline "Britain Rules Out Joining Single Currency Before Next Century," the *Washington Post* reported;

> "LONDON, Oct. 27—The British government today ruled out joining the European single–currency union until after the next national election early in the coming century, but Chancellor of the Exchequer Gordon

Brown said Britain should prepare to join soon after that if conditions appear favorable for the country's economy. Brown issued the government's most definitive statement yet on the politically treacherous subject of monetary union after a week of criticism in which he and other officials were accused of sending confusing signals on its intentions to financial markets and its European allies. The controversy threatened to undermine public support for the government of Prime Minister Tony Blair, which has enjoyed an extended honeymoon since its election last May. In making the announcement in the House of Commons, Brown sought to balance the government's pro–European posture and its enthusiasm for the principle of monetary union—scheduled to begin in early 1999—with the reality that current economic and political circumstances would not permit Britain to participate for perhaps five years."[28]

The announcement accomplished precisely what it was supposed to accomplish. The remainder of the planned financial acquisitions and mergers that had been announced were abruptly canceled until the situation clarified. Stock prices dropped for those companies, and large blocks of stock traded hands at bargain prices. Those companies whose mergers fell through thanks to Britain's announcement woke up the next morning much more vulnerable to takeover than they had been the night before. That set the stage for Step Three.

---

[28] Copyright © 1997 The Washington Post Company, October 27, 1997.

WHAT'S NEXT?

The US stock market still has some life left in it, and there is still considerable money to be made—both by investors and by the investment bankers who regularly collect their cut. Mergers between American companies and European companies have not yet run their full course. There are still many opportunities to consolidate power, wealth and control in the hands of those elite who believe the only way to keep the common man from destroying himself is by "taking the bull by the horns" themselves, but the bull market is still a little too strong to try and hog–tie just yet. Instead, it will have to exhaust some of its strength on its own. Although the bull market is strong, it isn't invulnerable. There are plenty of variables that could still tank the US market.

All of which are easily manipulated when the time comes. Here is a partial list of possible doomsday scenarios for the raging bull market of Wall Street as we approach the turn of the century and Europe's Project 2000.

- War: the Middle East is only one possible flash point. North Korea could easily launch an attack on the South that could trigger a dramatic market decline across the Asian financial markets. We've already seen what effect that could have on Wall Street.

- Oil Prices: the tensions in the Middle East and the potential for war could cause the price of oil to rise dramatically. An increase in demand among developed and developing nations over the next year or so could cause an increase in demand for energy that could create shortages every bit as severe as any cutback in the world's energy supply.

- A Manipulated Breakdown in World Trade: rising trade barriers, like those currently being erected between the US and Japan over the trade deficit, or the flap between the US and Europe over restrictions on imported beef, or the copyright violations and human rights issues that separate the US from China could curtail US access to these markets. This scenario could easily exhaust the bull by removing downward pressure on prices and reigniting inflationary pressures.

- Deflation: this is one of the most frightening scenarios. Downward price pressures from Southeast Asia increase demand for Asian products, at the expense of domestic manufacturing. Increased recessionary pressures in Southeast Asia could spread to Japan, causing a series of regional price devaluations. Price pressures there pull down prices elsewhere in the global economy. Once deflation takes hold, it has a curious effect. Reversing deflationary pressures is a little like turning a pickle back into a cucumber—it can't be done. Instead, you have to start over.

- Inflation: deflation's evil twin is still a possibility. The Fed views inflation as the biggest threat to the US market—with good reason. Full employment statistics create pressure to increase wages, as we have discussed elsewhere in this book. And that wage pressure is already here. That threatens to revive consumer inflation, which would have a chilling effect on the raging bull.

- Currency Crisis: this is one of the most easily manipulated of the possible doomsday scenarios.

Domestic inflation and trade deficits both have an effect on the strength of national currencies. The European Monetary Union plan, if all goes well, could upset the balance of trade even further. Goods which can be produced elsewhere cheaper than in the United States will attract more domestic consumers, hurting domestic sales. A stable, unified currency is the secret to America's economic success story. The fractured and unstable currencies of Europe are America's greatest strength. The EMU could well result in lower prices for European imports, and reduce demand for more expensive American exports. Any business owner knows that if your prices are too high, your competitor gets the orders.

A NEW CURRENCY

But there is one way to eliminate the currency fluctuation problem altogether. Europe has already made great strides in this direction. Eventually, the United States will follow, as will the rest of the world. It's a two–stage plan; first, the elimination of national currencies. All that is necessary is a stable, global currency unit. It may sound a little far fetched right now, but it is the only way to complete the cycle of globalization. In fact, without this eventuality, the entire global economic scheme must collapse under its own weight. Once Europe makes it "over the hump," the rest of the world will have to follow or lose any competitive edge. The European Currency Unit is the model, and will, in some form, become the world's benchmark currency. It may take a little time, but it is as certain as night following day. Remember, 20 years ago those "in the know" said a global economy was an impossibility. Today, it's reality, naysayers notwithstanding. A global currency is just as unthinkable…and just as inevitable.

A CURRENCY WITHOUT BACKING

For the last 70 years a monetary unit without any real value of its own has been in development. The backing of gold and silver was removed, eliminating the world's barter economy in favor of a debt–based system. The national currencies of the world are gradually moving toward a system in which the monetary unit is backed by the credit and property of its citizens. Most of the Asian nations found out just what that means in real terms following the great "Asian meltdown" of 1997. Many of them saw their currencies devaluate by as much as 70% because those currencies were not backed by anything of value. The same system exists in the United States, except the meltdown here will not come until Europe is ready. Until a global currency unit is prepared, it's unlikely the meltdown here will take place. The world economy still needs the US dollar as a benchmark to keep the system operating until the takeover is ready. But the currency itself has no intrinsic value of its own so the issuing authority is of no real consequence. Money is what people will accept in exchange for goods and services. It's just that simple.

A WORLD WITHOUT CASH

Once national economies are geared for a global currency unit, the actual issuance of currency itself becomes unnecessary. An electronic currency unit is all that is really necessary. Debit cards and value added cards are already in use in most places in the world—even in most Third World countries. Anyplace wired for telephone service and electricity can become a banking center by the simple expedient of adding an ATM machine. Most personal computers are already being used for direct banking operations. A user can connect to his or her bank, pay bills, transfer money, check account balances and do most of their banking without ever leaving the front of the computer screen. In the Developed World, most banks already require their customers to sign up for, at minimum, an ATM card. Direct deposit is common, especially for government checks like Social Security benefits or veteran's pensions. Most US government agencies are trying to force beneficiaries who don't have bank accounts to open them in order to collect benefits electronically. The argument is sound enough, it costs millions to print checks and mail them, pennies to transfer funds electronically. In this age of "reinventing government" to reduce government costs, such a plan is entirely sensible. In underdeveloped countries, the issuance of a value added electronic funds transfer card is not a big problem. Plans are in the works, via satelite, to connect even the most remote regions via cellular or digital communications systems. ATM's and card readers could theoretically operate in the middle of the Borneo jungle. The only mechanism yet to be established is the central bank of issue for a global currency unit. And that returns us to the European superstate and the fledgling Economic Currency Unit, not the US dollar. In order for a truly global economy to function, national currency exchange rates have to disappear. The currency speculators will disappear once all the profit has been squeezed out. They will be replaced by the profits gleaned by the central bank of issue, operated, of course, by those who set the operation in motion in the first place. Remember, those who believe in elitist rule are not evil, and neither are their plans. They mean to protect us from ourselves, and if they can make a little money in the process, well, why not? But the real objective is power, and the object of that power is to save us from wars, deprivation and want.

CHAPTER ELEVEN

THE MILLENNIUM BUG

"The more I read, the more convinced I am

that some economic disruptions are inevitable.

The year 2000 problem is a serious threat

to the global economy.

Yet it isn't being taken seriously enough."

EDWARD YARDENI,
DEUTSCHE MORGAN GRENFELL

To this point, most of the Plan has been gradual. Skillful planning, combined with fortuitous circumstances, creates its own luck, and, if you have the time and the money, the opportunity will create itself. As a general principle, there will always be a few die–hard individuals who will not "go gently into the good night" of a cashless, elitist global system of government. But what if that were the only choice? Suppose something could—overnight—end all government as we know it, without a shot being fired in anger? Enter the Millennium Bug, also known as the Y2K Problem. Y2K is difficult to explain—not because it is complicated, but because it is so simple. In fact, it boggles the mind to entertain the notion that it is merely an accident.

In the early days of computing, programmers, attempting to conserve as much operating system memory as possible, eliminated what they considered "unnecessary" information wherever possible. One place where they found they could save memory was in shortening the date from four digits to two digits. In today's computer world of extended RAM memory and high–powered Pentium (and beyond) CPU chips, it's difficult to imagine how removing two digits could make a significant difference. In the 1960s and 1970s computer storage space was so limited it was very expensive. Because dates are replicated over and over throughout programs, reducing the date by two digits was worth somewhere between $16 to 20 million per megabyte of storage space saved. Multiply that times the last 30 years. The bull market is largely a by–product of the computer revolution. Computers were made for the fractional reserve banking system, and the fractional reserve banking system was made for computers. As we've discussed, fractional reserve banking is when banks can lend up to ten times the amount of cash they have on reserve, inventing money that doesn't really exist until you pay it back. Before the advent of computers, inventing money was a tedious affair. When a bank in the reserve system invented more money, the information would have to entered in a ledger at the local level and approved up the line until finally the phantom money entered the Federal Reserve ledger book—at which point it officially "existed." It was a workable system, but it took time for the process to go from a loan application, up the line, and then back down again as money. Computers eliminated all that. Loans can be approved instantly, entries made simultaneously at every stop up and down the line, and the money appears on the loan officer's ledger immediately. He can then hand it to you. Before computers, there were no credit cards. The invention and development of banking computers made cheap money available immediately. With more money available, more would show up in the stock market, more quickly, making more money faster for investors. The money, as we have seen, isn't really money, it's computer–generated credit, always on the move from the bank to the investor to the market and back to the bank in the form of deposits. The difference is the individual investor's profit. If the money slowed down enough, it would be obvious that there really wasn't any, and the whole system might collapse. Computers keep that from happening by keeping the money in motion. The date and time between two transactions, even if it is only a matter of minutes or seconds, can be worth millions to whoever owns the money at a specific moment. For example, I borrow money from you at 10:00 a.m. I invest it by buying a stock that goes up 10% by 2:00 p.m. I sell, take my profit, and pay you back by 3:00 p.m. You've gotten your money back before the day even ended. I only owned it for four hours, but it was the right four hours. What if something happened where nobody was keeping track of the time?

AN ACCIDENT?

Industry apologists say the removal of the first two digits from the date was an understandable accident. Understandable to whom? It is difficult to accept the premise that computer programmers were unaware of the fact the Year 2000 would follow the Year 1999. They are, after all, computer programmers. By definition, especially in the early years, the entire focus of the industry was oriented to the future. It was necessary to design programs with an eye toward bigger, more powerful machines, especially mainframe computers. Programmers built in "steps" that would enable software and hardware to adapt to advances in technology, as well as meeting the expanding needs of the users for whom they were designing the systems. With all that attention being paid to the future, it strains the limits of credulity to accept the fact they forgot the future was going to happen! In the competition between programmers for bonuses and raises, it's at least possible it was an oversight. More likely, like politicians giving away entitlements that the next generation will have to pay for, they just didn't care. And to be fair to the programmers, it's not likely they believed that code written in the '60s would still be in use at the turn of the century. The problem with date codes is that every program uses them. Each time the date is accessed, it replicates the code, updating and performing calculations. One incorrect entry cascades through all the connected systems, and every calculation that follows is flawed. And each flaw builds on the one before, times millions and billions of lines of code. And the tasks those flawed bits of code are supposed to perform. It works like a virus, because that is what the Millennium Bug is—a built–in virus that threatens to wipe out 40 years of computerized records and shut down every computing system in operation.

THE BUG THAT ATE THE ECONOMY

What is being called "The Millennium Bug" is simply what will happen when the calendar turns over from 1999 to 2000. For example, December 31, 1999, would read 12/31/99. Therefore January 1, 2000, would be read by computers the world over as 01/01/00. And that's the problem! To a computer, that means January 1, 1900. Now, why should that be important? Let's consider a few things.

What if all the trains stopped running? And all the traffic lights quit working? And all the phones went haywire? If satellites quit transmitting, TV stations stopped broadcasting, planes quit flying, banks and the stock market shut down, and your electric coffee maker didn't start brewing when you told it to? And, worse than that, what if it happened all at the same time?

In the United States, the rail system is 100% computer dependent. Track schedules are maintained by computer. Meaning, the computer ensures that two trains don't come roaring down the same track from opposite directions. When the date rolls, the mainframe computers operating the nation's rail systems will think it is January 1, 1900. Therefore, a northbound train at 11:59 p.m. December 31, 1999 would disappear at the stroke of midnight! At least, as far as the computer is concerned. At 12:01 a.m. January 1, 2000, the mainframe would not expect that train to be there for another 100 years. What conductor would move his train under those circumstances?

Air traffic control computers could not accept flight plans for flights that originate on December 31, 1999, and are scheduled to land after midnight 2000. From the computer's point of view, that landing would have taken place 100 years before departure! Trains move food and necessities. Airliners move people. Without functioning computer systems, nothing moves anywhere. The aircraft themselves will be affected. Large airliners often have five hundred or more different on board computer systems governing everything from takeoffs and landings to navigational systems. All are date sensitive. In November 1997, KLM (Royal Dutch Airlines) became the first of what undoubtedly will be many airlines to announce they will ground their aircraft at midnight, December 31, 1999.

> "A set of crucial computers in the nation's air traffic control system should not be used beyond December 1999 because they may not operate reliably when the date rolls over January 1, 2000, and there is no way to predict the effect on air traffic, according to IBM, which built the computers."

It's hard to imagine more date dependent systems than federal entitlement programs. Dates of birth, dates of employment, dates of eligibility, etc., all become future at the stroke of 12:00, because the computer will believe it's 1900. All recipients will not yet have been born, contributed premiums, or be part of the system, when the internal calendar clicks over to 01/01/00. The problem is enormous, and there isn't nearly enough time to reprogram all the systems.

> "The General Accounting Office [warned] that the Social Security Administration (SSA) faces a possible computer crash in the year 2000 because the

agency has not started analyzing or fixing several crucial systems affected by the Year 2000 software glitch. Among the systems not yet analyzed are most of the 54 computer systems that operate state disability determination services, according to the GAO, the watchdog arm of Congress. The GAO also said the Social Security Administration has not developed adequate contingency plans in case its computers are not fixed in time. *The SSA has long been touted as the federal agency that is most keenly aware of the year 2000 problem* [emphasis mine]. The agency, whose mission critical systems collectively had been though to have about 34 million lines of computer code, began making year 2000 repairs almost a decade ago. 'If Social Security, which we've thought had everything under control, really doesn't, that raised new questions about other agencies,' said a Congressional staffer. According to the GAO, private contractors hired by the SSA to fix the year 2000 glitch on 42 of 54 state disability determination services computers discovered 33 million additional lines of code that need to be tested, and where necessary, fixed. Analyzing and fixing the problem likely will be a massive undertaking. In just one office, the GAO said it found 600,000 lines of code in 400 programs that operate the disability system."

Everyone is hoping some whiz kid will invent a "magic bullet" that will deal with the Millennium Bug in time. That makes as much sense as planning your budget based on lottery winnings—before the draw takes place. To fix the Y2K problem, mainly written in a now obsolete language called

COBOL, programmers need to search billions of lines of code, a line at a time, correcting each to recognize the new dates. It is estimated it would take 11,000 COBOL programmers three years to fix just the Social Security mainframe problems. At the time of this writing, there aren't that many available COBOL programmers in the whole world. All in all, it would take 300,000 COBOL programmers to fix just the US government's mainframes by the year 2000. And not all the mainframes are programmed in COBOL. Some are programmed in even lesser known archaic computer languages. The US Office of Management and Budget reported in 1997 that even the Federal Emergency Management Agency (FEMA), whose mission is to take over in a crisis, won't be on line after midnight, January 1, 2000! Try and look at it this way. Writing a single program that could repair the Y2K virus across all the platforms in which mainframes were programmed would be like discovering a single pill that could eliminate all the various mutations of the AIDS virus. Carrying the AIDS analogy even further, our magic pill would have to reverse all the damage already done, cure all the AIDS related diseases already ravaging victims, eliminate the possibility of re–infection, and inoculate everyone who is currently disease free. It would also have to identify all those whose infection is at the earliest stages and eliminate the virus before the victim even knew he was sick. Plus anticipate any possible mutations that might develop and eliminate those as well. It could happen, maybe. But nobody would willingly expose themselves to the AIDS virus based only on the hope that such a magic pill is just around the corner.

GREATEST CRISIS IN HISTORY?

A new joke making the rounds on the Internet would be much funnier if only it was less accurate. "If builders built houses the way programmers wrote programs, the first woodpecker would have destroyed civilization." It wouldn't be stretching the point to argue the Y2K problem could well become the greatest worldwide crisis in history. Without computers, the global economy would melt down faster than butter in a frying pan. Okay, you made your mortgage payment on December 15, 1999. Next one is due, oh, in about 100 years or so. Great for you, but what about the bank holding the note? Could you even sell your house after January 1, 2000? When is your car payment due again? Whose car does it become after midnight, January 1, 2000? And when did you say your savings bonds mature? Or your stocks, or whatever? If all the records say it's now 100 years ago, you are basically wiped out in every area where dates are an important element. Which is to say, everything you don't already own, you probably never will. All you've saved is locked away in a vault that won't open for 100 years.

> "Banks and other financial institutions generally will go bonkers if they don't fix the [Y2K] problem. In the worst case scenario, the entire financial infrastructure, including the stock market, will go haywire. Balances, records and transactions will be lost. Y2K could be the event that could all but paralyze the planet."

Here's just a tiny hint of what could happen—with just one tiny little bug gone mad. A little glitch in two of 145 AT&T frame relay switches shut down the AT&T's entire global ATM network in April, 1998. Although initially, only two frame relay switches failed, the cascade effect took over, and soon the entire network was down. During that outage, in excess of 5,000 corporations were unable to complete critical network–based business. Retailers were unable to authorize credit card payments, and financial institutions could not complete transactions. Engineers worked round the clock to locate the problem and fix it. Still, with only 145 frame relay switches to repair, locating the problem and going back on line took days. In business, seconds can make the difference between success and failure. In military situations, aircraft landings, etc., the difference between success and failure is measured in nanoseconds.

What happened then was a warning of what is to come. On January 1, 2000, computer systems will begin experiencing similar failures when mainframe computers will be unable to process dates.

Businesses that depend on delivery schedules to stay in business—won't. That doesn't just mean courier companies. Where is a McDonald's restaurant in Los Angeles going to get the beef to make hamburgers? There aren't too many cows walking down Wilshire Boulevard. Supermarket shelves will be empty by January 3 in most cities, and where will the replacement stocks come from? How will a trainload of milk cars get from Wisconsin to Los Angeles when nobody knows where the trains are? When service stations run out of gas, how will they get more? Without gas, the trucking system melts down. And so on. And so on. This is a crisis made to order—if you happen to be betting on the rapid development of a replacement system for the current world order. A new world order, if you will. A crisis that nobody—not the computer geniuses, not the government, not the world's collected scientific wisdom—nobody anticipated! A crisis that could be simply stated in this way. Nobody expected January 1, 2000, to follow December 31, 1999! A detail that somehow was overlooked!

SILENCE ISN'T ALWAYS GOLDEN

If there were nothing to fear from Y2K, then one would expect to hear reassuring words from our elected officials. After all, the surest way to forestall a panic is to announce that everything is under control. On the other hand, the surest way to start a panic is for the White House to announce that the "sky is falling." There has to be some balance. The truth behind the spin cycle right now can be found in the absence of comments altogether. At the time of this writing, President Clinton has spoken about 140 words in public dealing with Y2K. Vice President Al Gore has said exactly nothing—in keeping with his vice presidential record. Why is that, if there is nothing to worry about? America and the global economy is in denial. But because the problem is certain, and a catastrophic result imminent, the best anyone can say is nothing, while hoping the lemmings will keep pumping money into the market to cover the smart money's exodus.

> "This is potentially the most destructive part of the Year 2000 problem. This isn't the inconvenience part where your paycheck comes a few days late. This is the blood–in–the–streets–part."[29]

> "Every person that begins to understand the enormity of the disaster looming on the horizon will contribute

---

[29] *New York Times,* January 13,1998.

to growing awareness. But who will leave his/her money in the bank when it may be impossible to get your money the next day, or the next week? Who will not join the rush? Will you leave your money in your bank if there is more than a good chance you will not have access to it, due to computer lockup?"[30]

Who indeed? It's interesting to note just how few people are admitting in public what everyone in the know is saying privately.

"We have a very thin margin of tolerance to make this whole thing work. THERE IS NO PLAN B."[31]

BLIND AND DEFENSELESS

Unless a magic bullet is developed to deal with Y2K, it will take exactly one second for the world's leading military superpower to become a footnote in history. Operation Desert Storm showcased the US military's ultra high tech capabilities. Patriot missiles knocked Scuds from the sky—but not because the soldiers manning the missile batteries were good shots. Iraqi forces were sent running for their lives, thanks to US planes, missile systems, artillery, tanks and other high tech equipment. The ground war was little more than a "mopping up" operation. US planners initially expected thousands of American casualties. More than 20,000 body bags were among the millions of tons of equipment airlifted to Saudi Arabia in preparation for the transition from Operation Desert Shield to Operation Desert Storm. They weren't necessary. The Pentagon, flushed with success and seeing the opportunity to

---

[30] *Washington Post,* November 5, 1997.

[31] *Newsweek*, June 2, 1997, "The Day the World Shuts Down."

increase their budget, argued convincingly that the armed forces needed to expand the high tech arsenal even further. Smart weapons made up only 8% of the total ordinance in Desert Storm. In the 1998 Iraqi crisis, more than 90% of the weapons deployed were high tech, computer–controlled weapons systems. Operating these systems requires millions of computer software programs maintained by more than 200,000 software professionals. There are more than 30 billion lines of code that need to be examined and reprogrammed in order to keep the US military machine running one second past midnight on the last day of this century. Of the Department of Defense's 13,897 computer systems, at the time of this writing, exactly none of them are Y2K compliant. Congressional experts estimate it will take 21 years to repair just the most mission critical of these systems. Since Desert Storm, the US military has engaged in a massive downsizing campaign. One computer–operated weapons system is worth a division of combat riflemen. Unlike soldiers, these systems don't need to be paid, fed, housed or otherwise supported between wars. The Pentagon can just wheel them away to a closet somewhere until they become necessary. But when those systems go down (and they will, January 1, 2000, unless a computer miracle happens), those missing divisions of soldiers will be sadly missed. The much–vaunted US military machine, without its computers, will drop in the military pecking order to someplace below Russia, China, North Korea and even Cuba.

THE GREATEST CON JOB IN HISTORY?

The Y2K bug has only two possible explanations. The first, and most incredible, is that the collected wisdom of the greatest body of scientific knowledge in human history overlooked the fact that the 1900s would eventually come to a close. They just forgot!

The alternate explanation is not much more believable. Despite the overwhelming evidence that points to a global financial conspiracy among the movers and shakers at the top of the banker's food chain, it is hard to imagine that this is an engineered crisis. The most likely explanation is that the money trust simply recognized a fortuitous set of circumstances and capitalized on it accordingly. The evidence to support this conclusion can be found in the overwhelming apathy that surrounds the whole situation. Programmers—and banking CEO's and government officials—recognized the problem years ago. But until it started to get a little press, virtually nothing has been done to correct the problem in time! This is the most predictable disaster in history. If it impacts society to even a fraction of the degree expected, it will be the greatest global financial disaster in history, exceeding in magnitude even the Crash of '29! But nobody is doing much of anything about it. It is estimated that if all the programmers in the world began rewriting the code to make all the computers Y2K compliant beginning on January 1, 1998 and worked round the clock, three shifts, no days off or vacations, Y2K would be fixed sometime around 2005. Well, after everything crashes. Repairing Y2K is a multi–stage process that has no shortcuts.

First, diagnose the extent of the corruption. That means human beings reading billions of lines of code, locating every occurrence of abbreviated dates. Overlaying the defective code with a new program won't do the job. It will take human beings. Computers can only be taught to look for specific combinations; they can't intuitively identify which line of code contains distressed code. That takes human interaction.

One software developer said that at best, a diagnostic tool might be able to identify 30% to 40% of the code flaws—in some languages, like COBOL. Separate software would need to be developed for every one of the archaic computer languages that were used over the years. And identifying 40% of a virus means the remaining 60% will reinfect the system as soon as it is booted up! Once the code is identified, each individual line must be fixed. The repair is also a two–stage operation. First the offending codes must be rewritten, and then the rewrites have to be tested. After diagnosis and repair comes the most critical and time consuming stage of the operation. Testing. Nobody will have any idea whether or not the bug is squashed until the tests are all run. A missed repair could have effects ranging from reinfecting the whole system, producing unreliable calculations that will be even harder to find and fix, or, in a worst case scenario, causing the whole system to crash. Consultants recommend setting a target repair date of January 1, 1999, to allow a full year for testing. There just isn't time. Now, the bug was discovered several years ago—early enough to prevent a global meltdown by 2000. But very few systems managers have even begun to deal with the task at hand. Because the problem seems so simple, most assumed somebody would develop a piece of software that would do the job for them in time. There was not the hue and cry from the industry, the banks, or even the media that one would expect, given the predictable nature of the problem and the potential for catastrophe.

Social Security has been working on the Y2K bug since 1989. That begs an obvious question. If this was such a big surprise, something that everybody just forgot, shouldn't we be prosecuting the Social Security Administration for withholding critical information? Of course, I'm kidding. The Social Security Administration knew because everybody knew about Y2K long ago. It wasn't a surprise that this century would come to an end. That is merely the weakest excuse since the Nuremburg defendants claimed they were "just following orders."

Social Security is the only government agency with even a ghost of a chance of beating the Y2K deadline. Why is that? Could it be that the largest entitlement agency in the US needs to be functional in order to maintain control? How important will Social Security benefits be if that is the only source of income still operational? And how loudly will dissidents shout if they are risking that single source of income? And SSA isn't expected to be Y2K compliant in time, either. The question remains unanswered. If, with all the advance notice, considering the global implications, why didn't the money trust, which conceivably has the most to lose in a meltdown, insist that action be taken earlier? For the same reason they didn't announce the impending '29 disaster. There was money to be made then and money to be made in the event of another such catastrophe. In addition, it sets the stage perfectly for a reinvention of society more along the lines of rule by the elite. The United States President already has Executive Orders in the works to deal with Y2K by declaring a state of martial law. That seems to make some sense, considering the social breakdown that is sure to follow the food riots that are equally sure to follow the absolute collapse of our computerized world.

At the end of the day, it really doesn't matter whether it was the culmination of a carefully laid plan or the product of incomprehensible short–sightedness on the part of early software and hardware developers. The bottom line remains the same. A global meltdown of Biblical proportions is just a matter of time. And when it happens, it won't be the United States that picks up the pieces.

EUROPE—POINT, SET AND MATCH!

For much of this decade, Europe has been at a technological disadvantage, thanks to the breakup of the old Soviet bloc. Western Europe, which had just begun to make strides toward integrating the newest computer technology into its infrastructure, suddenly faced the added problem of absorbing the newly liberated, technologically challenged Eastern European bloc. As a result of this accident of history, Europe's technological advances stalled temporarily. The United States seized the opportunity to leap ahead. Unless Y2K is somehow neutralized, the advantage shifts to Europe. Even if one is willing to accept the "accident" theory—that Y2K was just an oversight—it worked out well for the Europlanners. The European money trust spent most of the last 200 years scheming for a way to seize back the "colonies." The worst case scenario for Y2K means a total meltdown in America. Thanks to the collapse of the Soviet Union, Europe is far less likely to suffer the effects of computer gridlock and is in much better position to pick up the pieces following a Y2K catastrophe. The Europeans have been busily engaged in preparing their own mainframe systems to be Y2K compliant and are much further along the way than the United States. At the current European pace of reprogramming, odds are that the Y2K bug's impact on Europe will be relatively minimal. Almost as if it were a plan coming together. It stretches a point to say the Millennium Bug was part of a master plan, but it is certainly a convenient coincidence.

CHAPTER TWELVE

CONCLUSION

Although the US market still has much to offer, its useful-
1997 ness to the global economy is waning. A tree cannot grow to
heaven, as we already know, but it can give shade to other
trees while they develop their strength and nourishment
from the leaves that fall from it. Eventually, however, the
smaller trees choke off the roots of the larger as they compete for room to grow. It all takes place under the surface,
but there are warning signs in advance.

There is a plan for a revived Europe, one that exceeds even
the most optimistic dreams of the conquerors of old who
attempted to unify Europe by force. Like the United States
before it, Europe is uniquely positioned to achieve maxi-
mum benefit from its own "manifest destiny" for greatness.
For the individual investor, that still means plenty of opportunity. Watch the European market closely. Keep an eye on
the multinational corporations and the big money managers,
those who handle pension funds, and the "untouchables"
like the great banking Houses: Morgan, Rockefeller, Schiff,
Kuhn, Loeb & Company, and others who own the largest
shares of stock in the Federal Reserve. Pay attention to the
signs. When the big money begins moving across the
Atlantic in large blocks, there is a reason. The warning signs
before the Crash of 1929 were clear and unmistakable, in
hindsight. But nobody was paying attention, because the
propaganda machine was in full swing, encouraging the
Key masses to ignore the obvious. Remember, history is like a
road map. If you know where you started, and are clear
where you are going, you can figure out where you are now.
The American economic miracle was born in Europe. It has
nearly run its course and will soon return, like a boomerang,
to where it began. America's economy will not cease to
exist, but it will certainly change direction. That direction

points directly to the European Economic Community of the next century. Our economics will be based entirely on what works for them, not us. And that brings us to our examination of the European situation, its goals, and America's ultimate financial destiny.

Just because Europe is set to emerge as the next superpower of the new Millennium does not mean that it will escape the coming financial apocalypse in the making. The trend seems to indicate a coming global deflationary spiral that will affect the economies of every political entity on earth. There have been at least two serious financial downturns every century since Shakespeare's father lost the farm. And, the crash of '29 is nothing compared to what is looming on the horizon. But this one, like 1929, is a managed crisis, and the ultimate beneficiaries have already been selected. The smart money isn't betting on Europe; it's grooming it. Remember the Golden Rule:

"He who has the gold makes the rules."

[handwritten] '06, '07 - '08 the global deflationary spiral is heavily upon us